Better Business Decisions Using Cost Modeling

Better Business Decisions Using Cost Modeling

For Procurement, Operations, and Supply Chain Professionals

Victor E. Sower and Christopher H. Sower

First published in 2011 by
Business Expert Press, LLC
222 East 46th Street, New York, NY 10017
www.businessexpertpress.com

ISBN-13: 978-160649-266-6 (paperback)

ISBN-13: 978-160649-267-3 (e-book)

DOI 10.4128/9781606492673

A publication in the Business Expert Press Supply and Operations Management collection

Collection ISSN: 2156-8189 (print)
Collection ISSN: 2156-8200 (electronic)

Cover design by Jonathan Pennell
Interior design by Scribe Inc.

First edition: September 2011

10 9 8 7 6 5 4 3 2 1

Printed in the United States of America.

Abstract

Information is power in supply chain operations, negotiations, continuous improvement programs, process improvement, and indeed in all aspects of managing an operation. Accurate and timely information can result in better decisions that translate into the improvement of bottom-line results. The development and effective use of cost modeling as a method to understand the cost of products, services, and processes can help drive improvements in the quality and timeliness of decision making. In the supply chain community, an understanding of the actual cost structures of products and services, whether with new or nonpartner suppliers, can facilitate fact-based discussions that are more likely to result in agreements that are competitively priced and with fair margins. Further, accurate cost models that are cooperatively developed between supply chain partners can form the basis for joint efforts to reduce non-value-added costs and provide additional focus toward operational improvement.

While many organizations feel confident that they have an understanding of the cost structure for products and services produced internally, cost modeling often uncovers areas where significant cost improvement can be obtained. Cost-of-quality is a particular type of internal cost model that analyzes the true costs associated with the production of less than perfect products and services. The development of a cost-of-quality model can provide insight into how products or services of higher quality can be produced at lower cost.

This book provides the business professional a concise guide to the creation and effective use of both internal and external cost models. Development of internal cost models is discussed with illustrations showing how they can be deployed to assist in new product development, pricing decisions, make-or-buy decisions, and the identification of opportunities for internal process improvement projects. The creation and use of external cost models are discussed, providing insight into how their use can drive collaborative improvement efforts among supply chain partners, better prepare for price negotiations, and keep negotiations focused on facts rather than emotions—all while allowing for future discussions with preferred suppliers to focus on more strategic and operational improvement initiatives and less on pricing. A number of detailed examples are provided to illustrate how cost models are constructed and to demonstrate how they have been effectively deployed.

Keywords

Cost model, Should-cost model, projected cost model, crossover model, cost of quality, purchasing, negotiation, cost management, strategic sourcing, procurement, Excel applications, supply chain management, make or buy, non-value-added cost reduction, breakeven, learning curve, total cost of ownership, net present value

Contents

Illustrations

Tables

Figures

Examples

Acknowledgments

The authors would like to acknowledge the peer reviewers for this book for their careful review and helpful comments:

Dr. Ross Lovell, Professor Emeritus of Operations Management, Sam Houston State University

Mr. Peter Birkholz, Management Consultant—Birkholz Management Co., LLC

Mr. David Maley, Vice President Procurement.

Mr. Rick Monical, Chief Procurement Officer, BP Azerbaijan

Dr. Jaideep Motwani, Professor and Chair, Department of Management, Grand Valley State University

We would like to thank Mr. Scott Isenberg, principal and consultant, CounselPub Publishing Services, who provided us the opportunity to undertake the writing of this book, and the editorial staff at Business Expert Press for their excellent work in expertly taking our work from manuscript to finished product.

Lastly we would like to acknowledge and thank our wives Judy and Emilie for their support and encouragement.

Abbreviations and Acronyms

ABC	activity-based costing
BEP	breakeven point
BLS	Bureau of Labor Statistics
BOL	bill of labor
BOM	bill of material
COGS	cost of goods sold
COQ	cost of quality
COS	cost of service
CPI	Consumer Price Index
ERP	enterprise resource planning
FC	fixed cost
FDC	factory direct cost
FMCSA	Federal Motor Carrier Safety Administration
FOB	free on board
FOIA	Freedom of Information Act
GM	gross margin
GPU	gross profit per unit
HR	human resource
IRS	Internal Revenue Service
JIT	just-in-time
MRB	materials review board
MRO	maintenance, repair, and operating
MTM	methods time measurement
NAICS	North American Industry Classification System
NPV	net present value
PAF	prevention, appraisal, failure quality cost model
P&L	profit and loss statement
PPI	Producer Price Index
PV	production volume
QA	quality assurance
R&D	research and development
RFI	request for information
RFP	request for proposal

RISI	Resource Information Systems, Inc.
RMA	Risk Management Association
SG&A	sales, general, and administrative expense
OCC	standard occupational code
SOP	standing operating procedure
SPC	statistical process control
SOW	statement of work
tmu	time measurement unit
TCO	total cost of ownership
TR	total revenue
VC	variable cost

CHAPTER 1

Introduction

Watch the costs and the profits will take care of themselves.

—Andrew Carnegie

In God we trust; all others must bring data.

—W. Edwards Deming

Efficiency and effectiveness in procurement, supply chain operations, and internal operations are important to the success of all organizations. This book discusses a variety of external and internal cost models that, when used properly, can help an organization dramatically reduce costs of both purchased and internally produced goods and services. There are numerous examples in the chapters that follow—most from the authors' experience—of how organizations saved substantial amounts through the use of cost modeling. One organization saved more than $1 million annually on a single purchasing contract negotiation through the use of external cost modeling. Another reduced its cost of production by more than 6% in less than 6 months through the use of internal cost modeling. What might your organization save by using cost modeling?

The benefits of cost modeling extend beyond the purchase price to long-term costs of ownership, safety, risk management, and to overall viability of product lines and businesses. But use of the models alone has no effect on costs. It is the improved management decisions that are based on the information provided by cost models that reduce costs. So in addition to discussing how to create cost models, this book illustrates ways the results of the fact-based information output of the cost models can be presented and used to enhance decision quality.

We have all heard the expression "Information is power." Power, as used here, does not refer to coercive power, although the results of cost modeling can be used in a coercive way. But coercion is not the only form of power, nor is it the best. The use of coercive power might result in a one-time "win," but it will not result in a long-term change in behavior. Power based on factual information is more likely to result in short- and long-term benefits to all parties. Power in the form of actionable information is necessary in order to get things done and thus has a place in collaborative supply chain relationships as well as in operations internal to the organization. Indeed, a number of studies[1] have shown the positive influences of power on procurement and supply chain performance.

Cost issues can be better addressed with external parties using information rather than coercion. In procurement, the knowledge provided by an external cost model increases the purchaser's relative power in price negotiations and can help assure that the final price paid is fair to both supplier and purchaser. Additionally, the information provided by an external cost model can be shared with supply chain partners to serve as the basis for discussions directed toward collaborative efforts to reduce costs throughout the supply chain. This transparency can benefit all supply chain members.

Example 1.1. External Projected Cost Models in Price Negotiations

Supplier A's representative is meeting with her client's purchasing manager about the renewal of the contract for purchase of materials from Supplier A. "As you know, transportation and energy costs have risen dramatically since our last negotiation. In addition, we have seen increases in many other cost categories as well. As a result we must ask for a price increase of 15% for the new contract period." We have all been there. The question is, will the price negotiations progress much like those with a vendor in a flea market, or will they be fact based and focused on achieving a deal that is fair to both parties?

In a flea market, the vendors have all the information. They know their costs and they know what prices shoppers at last Saturday's market were willing to pay. The vendor starts with a price he believes is higher than you are willing to pay, and you counter with a price lower than you believe the vendor will accept. After several rounds of discussion, if you have not agreed on a price somewhere in the middle, you begin to walk away. Now the real negotiations begin. No matter what price you pay, you feel as if you have been taken advantage of. This is no way to negotiate prices in the current business environment.

How would the negotiations with Supplier A's representative differ if you had an accurate estimate of the supplier's product cost and a feeling for what a fair profit should be? Instead of countering the supplier's offer with a lowball offer of your own, hoping to meet in the middle, you might counter by saying, "This is what we believe your cost for this product to be. Adding a profit margin based on the industry average, we believe the increase in price should be just 8% instead of 15%." The supplier may well respond that your cost estimates are incorrect. Your response is, "Show me where I am wrong." We are now engaged in fact-based negotiations and are much more likely to arrive at a price that is fair to both parties.

Where do we obtain the information about supplier cost? We construct an external cost model. Information is power, and cost modeling can empower you.

Similarly, discussions about ways to improve internal operations always proceed more smoothly and with a greater probability of success when based on objective information rather than on opinion and speculation. The knowledge provided by an internal cost model increases the ability of an organization to identify areas where improvement efforts can be best focused to increase the price competitiveness of products and services produced by the organization. Internal cost models are also of value in new product and process development to evaluate feasibility and aid in pricing decisions.

Human/Political Issues

Human issues can be especially important, particularly when using internal cost models with internal customers (the people within our organization who receive our work or services) and external cost models with supply chain partners. Simply presenting the results of a model in a meeting and expecting everyone to see the logic of your recommendation rarely works. More frequently this out-of-the-blue style of presentation will result in some sort of push back or defensive reaction. When the buy-in of external constituents or internal customers is required to build on the results of a cost model, it is important to involve those constituents from the beginning of the modeling project. When those involved feel that they are part of a cooperative effort that involves cost modeling, the probability of buy-in is greatly increased. On the other hand, when people feel that others are encroaching on their turf, they often will resist acting on the most objective evidence supporting that action.

Working with an internal customer to fully understand both the quantitative and nonquantitative aspects of a cost-saving opportunity will help assure the quality of the model and the acceptance of the results. For example, working with store management to understand the aesthetics of lighting as well as the costs associated with that lighting will help assure that the lower-cost lighting alternatives being modeled will satisfy the aesthetic requirements. Involving store management from the beginning makes it "our" cost modeling project and enhances the probability that everyone will accept the recommendations resulting from the model.

The General Cost Model: What Should the Cost of a Specific Product or Service Be?

In this book we discuss two general categories of cost model: external cost models and internal cost models. Cost modeling may generally be defined as the analysis of resource data including direct labor, direct material, indirect cost, sales, general and administrative (SG&A) costs, research and development (R&D) cost, and profit to understand the projected or true cost of products and services produced or purchased by the organization. It is a critical procurement tool that can provide "the foundation for virtually everything that a purchasing organization does, from setting strategy, to simplifying designs, to improving supplier operations and negotiating piece prices."[2] The general cost model is depicted in Figure 1.1.

External cost modeling's main purpose is the evaluation of the reasonableness of a price or quotation for a product or service; however, often other cost drivers relating to how the company's operations inadvertently add to supplier costs and thus the end price may be identified from the modeling process. Identification of these customer-based cost drivers can cost model is useful in projecting costs for products and services under development and for analyzing the cost structure for existing products and services to determine fruitful areas for cost improvement activities. It is generally true that improvement activities are more likely to be successful when the parameters of interest (in this case cost parameters) are well defined and measureable.

The development of cost models alone will not produce a more effective and efficient organization. The results obtained are dependent on an organization and its management adopting a culture that integrates them into the decision-making process. That culture shift combined with appropriate development and use of cost models will result in better management decisions that will positively affect effectiveness and efficiency.

Interestingly, it is neither as difficult to construct an external cost model nor as easy to construct an internal cost model as one might expect. There are many sources of information available to support external cost modeling. Many of these sources are readily searchable online. Examples include government census data and information available through industry associations. While most if not all the information required to construct an internal cost model already exists within the organization, rarely is it sufficiently accurate, at the necessary level of detail, or in the appropriate form to be used directly. Frequently the model builder must drill down through several layers to find the information required and then must validate that information to assure its accuracy before using it to construct the model. We discuss the process of creating cost models and data sources for those models in chapter 2.

Categories and Uses of Cost Models

In this book we discuss two general categories of cost models: external and internal. Within each general category, there are multiple specific types of cost models as will be shown in the following list. In chapter 3 we discuss internal-projected cost models. An internal-projected cost model is used to understand the cost structure of products and services produced within your organization to aid in decision making. Among the uses for internal-projected cost models is cost feasibility analysis for new product/service development by providing a snapshot of the projected costs to produce a specific product or service. The learning curve cost model is discussed as a way to adjust the basic model for increased labor efficiency expected to be derived over time. These models are useful as inputs to pricing decisions for new products and services. Another use of internal cost models is to identify opportunities for reducing costs and increasing efficiency. One example in chapter 3 works through the cost model a manufacturing company used to help reduce the factory direct cost of one class of products by more than 6% over a 6-month period.

Internal and External Cost Models

- Internal cost models
  - Internal-projected cost model
  - Basic breakeven cost model
  - Stepped breakeven cost model
  - Make-or-buy cost models
  - Crossover chart model
  - Cost-of-quality model
- External cost models
  - Industry-specific projected cost models
    - Product
    - Service
  - Total cost of ownership model

Other types of internal cost models are discussed in chapter 4. Each type is designed for a particular purpose. Often several types of internal cost models are used during the life of a project to guide different types of decisions. Breakeven cost models can be used to determine the relationship between sales volume, expressed as total revenue; fixed costs of production; and variable costs of production. Breakeven models are useful in new product/service development for determining the sales volume necessary to reach breakeven and thus provide a lower bound on project feasibility. The basic breakeven model is suitable for a limited range of production. The stepped breakeven model allows for analysis over an unlimited range of production. Next we discuss an internal cost model that compares the variable cost of internal production to quotations for outside production by a supplier that is useful to support make-or-buy decision making. The crossover chart is a type of internal cost model that is related to the breakeven model. It is useful in process selection and make-or-buy decisions by identifying the range of total cost over which specific options are preferred.

The cost-of-quality model is an internal cost model that is very useful in quality management. This model achieves a level of granularity not found in most standard cost systems. The increased granularity facilitates the identification of specific areas where costs are incurred due to poor quality. In most standard cost systems, much of this information is buried within variance and overhead accounts. The typical reaction for an organization using cost-of-quality modeling is incredulity, because without the model they had significantly underestimated their costs due to poor quality.

Certain internal cost models are most useful in the early stages of the product or service life cycle where the focus is on feasibility and pricing. Other models are most useful during the middle stages of the product or service life cycle where the emphasis is on increasing output and efficiency and lowering cost. However, all types of internal cost models can be used effectively to support decision making in all phases of the product or service life cycle.

In chapters 5 and 6, we discuss external cost models. Specifically, we discuss industry-specific cost models for both products (chapter 5) and services (chapter 6). The primary example used in chapter 5 demonstrates how a retailer saved more than $1 million per year on corrugated boxes using cost modeling. The primary example used in chapter 6 shows how another firm used cost modeling to save more than $12 million over the 3-year life of a transportation services contract.

In chapter 7 we discuss a particular type of cost model referred to as the total cost of ownership (TCO) model. TCO models are critical components of strategic sourcing activities because they help the purchaser look beyond the initial price when making the purchase decision. When the total costs associated with a purchasing decision over the life of the product or service purchased are explicitly examined using TCO modeling, the purchasing decision often will be different than the decision that results from an analysis that focuses exclusively on the initial price.

Cost models provide a snapshot of a particular cost component for a particular point in time usually to support a specific decision. However, if it is desirable to track that cost component over time, this may be done simply by updating the model. While specialized cost modeling software is available, a properly constructed cost model using a spreadsheet can facilitate the updating of the model. Periodically updating the model is particularly useful when the original use of the model involves setting cost improvement goals by providing a series of snapshots that enable the tracking of progress toward the goal.

Cost models are tools that can provide additional power to enable managers to increase organizational efficiency through lower costs and increase organizational effectiveness through better quality decisions. The models are useful in negotiations with suppliers by helping to keep the discussions focused on facts rather than on opinion and political maneuvers. The appropriate use of cost modeling can increase supply chain effectiveness and efficiency by facilitating collaborative efforts among supply chain partners to decrease costs and improve performance. Cost modeling should be part of every supply chain, procurement, and operations professional's toolbox.

CHAPTER 2

Constructing Cost Models

You have to start with the truth. The truth is the only way that we can get anywhere, because any decision-making that is based upon lies or ignorance can't lead to a good conclusion.

—Julian Assange

In chapter 1 we defined cost modeling as the analysis of resource data including direct labor; direct material; indirect cost; sales, general, and administrative (SG&A) costs; research and development (R&D) cost; and profit to understand the projected or true cost of products and services produced or purchased by an organization. But in the broadest sense, a cost model may be defined simply as a fact-based tool created with all the various cost components to assist business professionals with decision making. Cost modeling requires a basic understanding of financial principles, cost accounting, and the operations or industry to be modeled. This chapter provides an overview of the overarching principles and the best practices necessary to create sound cost models. Some of these foundational principles we review include financial principles, conceptual designs, architecture and construction, auditability, fitness for purpose, and the various data sources used to construct the models.

Foundational Principles

Cost modeling starts with process mapping from raw materials to product delivery/service performance. Financial expertise is then needed for the modeler to incorporate the data collected into a financial model to assist in decision making. Specifically, a thorough understanding of income statements, profit and loss (P&L) statements, cost accounting, and to a lesser degree, balance sheets is required to create good cost models. Whether modeling the cost of a potential project, internal operation, or a supplier-provided product or service, a sound grounding in basic financial principles is necessary, as well as a thorough understanding of how to apply that knowledge to use operational data to quantify the cost of that activity.

Income statements are utilized by all business organizations to understand the profit or loss achieved in particular business operations. Similarly P&L statements are essentially the same as income statements but are designed for internal use and thus do not reflect tax costs. While all business professionals should be familiar with the purpose and use of income statements, those not directly working in the fields of accounting or finance may not have the same level of experience analyzing them. There are many books and publications that provide greater in-depth insight into the analysis of financial statements, but because income statements and P&Ls form the backbone for all the cost models discussed in subsequent chapters, a high-level explanation and definition of key terms is provided.

At the most basic level, income statements contain the components comprising the general cost model discussed in chapter 1 (Figure 1.1) and listed in Table 2.1.

Additional income statement terms that need to be understood in cost modeling are cost of goods sold (COGS), cost of service (COS),

Table 2.1. Income Statement Components and Definitions

Income statement component	Definition
Revenue (sales)	Total of all sales dollars for a specified time period
Direct labor	Total cost of laborers directly involved in the production of the product/service sold
Direct material	Total cost of all materials encompassed in the product sold
Indirect costs (sometimes referred to as overhead)	All other costs associated with producing the products and services (equipment amortization/depreciation, electricity/gas, repairs, inspection labor, supervisory labor, etc.)
SG&A	Total indirect expenses not directly associated with producing the products and services (advertising, executive salaries, sales returns and allowances, sales staff compensation, etc.)
R&D	Total indirect expenses related to R&D activities
Income taxes	Taxes paid on any net profits before taxes
Net profit after taxes	Profit remaining after subtracting cost of goods sold, SG&A, R&D, and income taxes from revenue

gross profit, gross profit percentage, and net profit percentage. In the production of goods, COGS encompasses all the direct costs attributable to the production of that product. Similarly, COS is composed of all the direct costs attributable to providing a service (i.e., little or no direct material costs). Gross profit is measured as the dollar value to the business when subtracting COGS (or COS) from revenue. These basic financial measures may be calculated from basic income statement data as follows:

1. COGS = direct labor + direct material + indirect costs
2. COS = direct labor + indirect costs
3. Gross profit = revenue – COGS (or COS in service industries)
4. Gross profit percentage = gross profit ÷ revenue
5. Net profit = revenue – gross profit – SG&A – R&D – income taxes
6. Net profit percentage = net profit ÷ revenue

A strong working knowledge of financial statements is one foundational building block for creating cost models, but another pivotal piece is an understanding of activity-based costing (ABC). ABC may be narrowly defined as a method of reassigning costs accurately from general cost categories to specific cost objects associated with specific outputs, processes, products, services, or customers.[1] ABC analyses are applied to manufacturing and service settings to provide management insight into the actual costs associated with particular activities. Example 2.1 provides an illustration of how activities are equated to costs under the ABC methodology. The examples used in this chapter are based on one of the author's experiences; however, the actual data have been disguised to further protect the company's identity.

Example 2.1. XYZ Apparel

A specialty apparel retailer, XYZ Apparel, is interested in understanding the time required for store associates to unfold, hang, and steam garments to prepare them for display on the sales floor. As a part of the cost analysis, the corporate store operations manager hires a third-party consulting firm to assess several key areas in a sample of stores.

The deliverables the consultant is required to provide include process maps of what is occurring at store locations and the times associated with those activities.

The consulting firm reports the following findings to the corporate store operations manager:

- Mean time to unfold garment = 5 seconds
- Mean time to hang garment = 15 seconds
- Mean time to steam garment = 60 seconds
- Total mean time for activities = 80 seconds/garment
- Total garments unfolded, hung, and steamed = 800
- Calculated total time for all garments unfolded, hung, and steamed = 17 hours and 47 minutes
- Total store associate hours for the week = 120 hours

The corporate store operations manager knows the mean wage for store associates including benefits is \$12.25/hour. Based on this activity analysis, she is now able to report the following:

- Each garment costs \$0.272 to unfold, hang, and steam in the store.

$$\frac{80 \text{ seconds / garment}}{60 \text{ seconds}} \times \frac{12.25 \text{ / hour}}{60 \text{ minutes}} = \$0.272$$

- In total, this activity consumed 17 hours and 47 minutes of productivity.

$$\frac{80 \text{ seconds / garment}}{60 \text{ seconds}} \times \frac{800 \text{ garments}}{60 \text{ seconds}} = 17 \text{ hours, 47 minutes}$$

- The productivity time accounts for \$217.78 in store associate labor.

$$17.78 \text{ hours} \times \$12.25/\text{hour} = \$217.78$$

- In total, this activity accounted for 14.8% of store associate time.

$$\frac{17.78 \text{ hours}}{120 \text{ Total associate hours}} = 14.8\%$$

Equipped with this information, the corporate store operations manager now has the first piece to begin collecting quotations from overseas suppliers to try to determine whether there is a financial benefit to have this activity performed at the factory rather than at the store and to have the garments shipped already on hangers.

Example 2.1 provides an illustration of the analysis of labor costs; however, the same methodology may be used to understand equipment costs. The amortization and depreciation expenses incurred on production equipment can be easily allocated to specific units based on the time consumed for production and setup activities. This allows the operations managers to provide more accurate cost estimates for production of quoted units to their sales teams. In turn, this assists in ensuring that one customer's product does not subsidize the cost of another, and the organization can be more competitive while remaining profitable.

The ability to convert time into cost is a central principle of cost modeling, as costs incurred must be recouped whether they are from internal operations or external suppliers. Conducting these types of studies to assign costs to activities removes the mystery of the impact a particular activity has on the operational costs for a product or service. Additionally, this information provides the operations managers with essential information necessary to drive efficiencies and reduce total cost. These concepts are examined in greater detail in chapter 3.

Conceptual Design

The construction of cost models should always begin with a conceptual design phase. The conceptual design phase begins with the central question, "What are we attempting to model?" The best cost models are generally the brainchild of strong cross-functional teams, so accuracy depends on the alignment of purpose and objectives for what is being modeled.

When addressing the clarity of purpose around "what" the team is attempting to model, the immediate follow-up question is, "What data or information is required to create the model?" Framework sessions are beneficial in determining the necessary questions to ask, as well as identifying outside influences or uncertainties that may need to be incorporated into the model to assess risk. A framework session may be defined as a meeting of the minds to understand all areas in need of analysis for a particular project or model formation. Framework sessions begin with the team identifying and collecting all potential issues or concerns regarding the business or decision the team is looking to model. Example 2.2 shows the issues identified during the XYZ Apparel team's framework session.

Example 2.2. Framework Session Issues

Building upon the earlier example of the store operations manager working for a specialty apparel company, the corporate store operations manager and the cross-functional team for XYZ Apparel conducted a framework session to ensure that all cost elements, decision factors, and uncertainties were identified for inclusion in the cost model. Fifteen cost elements were identified during the session to be considered as part of any cost model and subsequent recommendation.

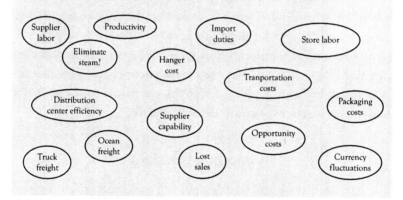

Once all issues are identified, an influence diagram can be constructed to determine the relationship each issue has on the value proposition the team is attempting to model. Influence diagrams are tools utilized early in projects to show the relationships of all the components identified in framework sessions and their relative influence on the value proposition. Often greater insight is gleaned through this process, which results in the addition of new components to the model as shown in Example 2.3.

Example 2.3. Influence Diagram

After the cross-functional team identified all the uncertainties and decision factors, they developed an influence diagram to illustrate the impact of each element relative to the value proposition being modeled. The arrows show the direction of the influence. For example, supplier labor is shown to influence productivity in the diagram. In this case, two new components were identified and added as a result of constructing the influence diagram.

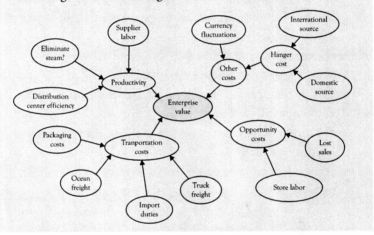

At this point it is useful to create specific questions relating to the component details, the answers to which will provide the information necessary to populate the cost model. Some of the questions for the XYZ Apparel example are illustrated in Example 2.4.

Example 2.4. Component Details

The corporate store operations manager and the team continue to build upon the cost information already collected to determine the potential value of shifting the unfolding, hanging, and steaming activities from the stores to an overseas supplier. To ensure all team members are cognizant of the meaning of the cost elements, the team creates questions to correspond with each component of the influence diagram created. Obtaining answers to these questions, the team believes, will provide the information needed to populate the cost model to better understand this opportunity.

- What is the labor rate for the supplier to provide this service? Is this labor as efficient as store labor?
- Could steaming be eliminated altogether if garments were shipped on hangers?
- What would be the productivity level of supplier workers compared to store personnel?
- Are our garment suppliers capable of shipping garments on hangers? Is it as cost efficient?
- Is there a cost difference to shipping garments on hangers compared to flat/folded (ocean freight, truck freight, import duties, packaging)?
- If garments are shipped with hangers from overseas, do we avoid separate hanger shipment costs?
- Will our distribution centers see productivity gains or losses with a potential switch?
- What currency fluctuations come into play when considering this switch?
- Is the store procuring or scheduling incremental labor to perform the unfolding, hanging, and steaming activities?
- Is there an opportunity cost to performing these activities in the store (i.e., less customer face time results in lost customer sales)? Or could we reduce store associate hours?

The benefit of the framework session is to provide a full vetting of all potential influencing factors on the subject to be modeled. Without these sessions the modeler is likely to neglect some key items of interest to the business and have an incomplete model that requires revision and rework, or worse, the modeler is likely to recommend a decision that does not consider all the critical success factors. The primary purpose of cost models is to enhance decision quality, and creating models in the absence of a framework jeopardizes the model's integrity and purpose. It is during framework sessions that the team can delineate what level of detail is necessary to ensure with a high degree of confidence the precision and accuracy of the model.

Architecture and Construction

With the influence diagram firmly defined, the next step is to determine the tool that will be utilized to create the cost model. Some organizations may have internally developed tools or may have acquired licenses for cost estimation software specific to their business. However, for the purposes of this book, we will assume no specialized software exists. In the absence of an already developed program, the most prevalently used cost model development tool is a spreadsheet. The spreadsheet used to illustrate this book is Microsoft Excel.

All cost models, whether constructed using a spreadsheet or specialized cost modeling software, need to have a well-defined architectural structure with a clear and logical flow and auditability. Professional programmers never begin to write even a single line of code without a well-defined roadmap and architecture. Similarly, cost models in the conceptual phase should not bypass the design phase and go directly into construction.

Though there is no singular best practice published relating to the actual design of a cost model, there are some consistent elements around development that should be followed. The elements the creator should be cognizant of when building the architecture of the cost model include usability, auditability, and fitness for purpose.

Usability has great importance when constructing cost models. If the user interface of the cost modeling tool is overly complex, it may deter the business from utilizing it to its fullest potential. With that thought in mind, when building a cost model utilizing a spreadsheet, creating a single tab (i.e., a single spreadsheet in a workbook of spreadsheets) for the user interface is highly recommended. The components that should be present in this tab of the spreadsheet are any variables you wish to manipulate. Typically these variables are separated into "assumption variables" and "decision variables." Assumption variables would be any components not under the direct control of the company but that have significant influence on the outcome being modeled. These variables would include items such as currency fluctuations, interest rates, import duties, and commodity prices. Decision variables, on the other hand, are components the company has direct influence over. Decision variables may include the following: make-or-buy, transportation mode, production volume, and price point. Though assumption and decision variables are to be located on the same tab of the dashboard/user interface worksheet, they should reside in separate, clearly labeled areas of the sheet. This will allow the business to conduct scenario testing based on assumption and decision variables together and independently. Example 2.5 provides an illustration of how the dashboard/user interface for XYZ Apparel in the example case might look using Excel. An updated view of the dashboard will be seen later in the chapter as outputs are incorporated.

Auditability refers to the integrity and transparency of the cost model created. Not unlike studies conducted in the scientific community, cost models should have clearly documented logic that can be replicated. Failure to document adequately creates confusion for both the model builder and anyone trying to understand the model. Subsequently, this can lead to questions about the model's accuracy and applicability. Clearly documenting the structure allows for model revisions and improvements while providing any evaluator a clear ability to follow the logic of the model.

When constructing cost models within a spreadsheet environment, the auditability can be improved markedly by implementing a number of key best-practice techniques. Chief among these is to avoid referencing outside workbooks—that is, separate spreadsheets and files. Links to outside workbooks are difficult to follow, and if the structure, cell reference, or location of that workbook were to change, the tool would no longer function. Second, never reference cells in a spreadsheet by their cell address location (e.g., C43). Instead, name cells and cell ranges in a consistent format that allows you to distinguish assumption variables, decision variables, and calculated fields. Naming cells and ranges in a meaningful manner allows the user to easily understand the formulas present in the model. Further, do not "hard code" values into formulas for calculation purposes; instead, make the hard-coded value an input on your user interface (either an assumption variable or decision variable). For example, if an interest rate of 7% is assumed within the model, the 7% should be a variable referenced from another input source in the formula. Inputting the percentage directly into the formula makes it difficult to audit and ensure adjustments are easily made if assumptions change. Lastly, work to keep all calculations in the model on a single tab in the workbook. This can prove challenging, but avoiding multiple tabs of calculations can greatly improve visibility into the inner workings of the cost model.

Example 2.5. Dashboard/User Interface Tab

Decision Variables

Make vs. Buy	Buy
Packaging	On Hanger
Transporation mode	Ocean

Assumption Variables

		UOM
Labor rate	$12.25	Hour
Lost sales	5%	
Currency exchange (Chinese Yuan to USD)	6.61	Yuan
Interest rate	5.75%	
Import duties (based on packaging—impacts goods classification)	12.50%	
Transportation expenses (based on modal decision)	$2,500	Container
Packaging costs (based on packaging decision)	$1.53	Carton

Dark gray fields vary with decision variables
Light gray fields are user-input variables

Making navigation of the model within the tool easy is not sufficient to make it auditable. An additional tab should be created within the workbook that includes the model's purpose, the architectural design of the workbook (all tabs and their relation to one another), the influence diagram, any formatting conventions utilized, the version of the model, the model designer's name, and the latest revision date. Example 2.6 illustrates how the corporate store operations manager for XYZ Apparel might use an Excel tab to outline information about the cost model. Note that each box in Example 2.6 represents a distinct and separate tab of an integrated workbook.

Example 2.6. About the Model Tab

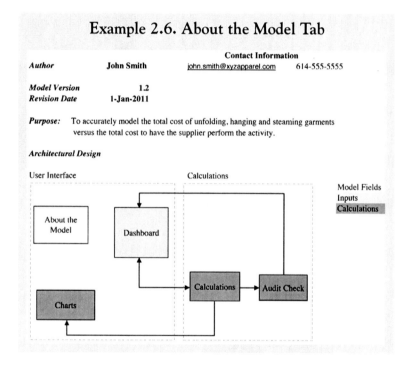

Contact Information

Author   **John Smith**   john.smith@xyzapparel.com   614-555-5555

Model Version   1.2
Revision Date   1-Jan-2011

Purpose: To accurately model the total cost of unfolding, hanging and steaming garments
            versus the total cost to have the supplier perform the activity.

Architectural Design

Fitness for purpose refers to the model's ability to provide the output necessary to assist in decision making. Now that the model is created, inputs are ready for entry, and the calculations have been tested and shown to work as designed, the output of the model must be represented. The best scenario is to keep the output on the same tab of the spreadsheet as the input so that the user has a "dashboard" feel for the tool. This dashboard should dynamically update as changes are made in the assumption variables and decision variables, so ensure any charts and pivot tables created maintain those cell references. All the information presented in report form on the dashboard should be significant to management needs and assist in the decision-making process.

Example 2.7 shows the manner the corporate store operations manager and the XYZ Apparel team chose to display results of their cost model.

The key take-away from cost model construction is that the output of the cost model should be of sufficient detail so that not only can the team make a recommendation to leadership but also the impact on each area of the business is identified from an operations and costing perspective. In the example with XYZ Apparel, the team's illustration of general ledger line impact is important to note. Were this level of detail not provided, variances in these general ledger accounts would not have easily identifiable explanations.

Data Sources

Understanding the concepts, techniques, and best practices of constructing cost models provides the framework for construction. However, even the most intricate cost models are only as good as their inputs. Stealing a common phrase used by programmers, "garbage in, garbage out" very much applies to the world of cost modeling as well. The cost model created may pass all auditable checklists, but if the validity or reliability of the data is questionable, the decision quality will suffer. Ensure data sources utilized are reputable and reference them within your model assumption variables.

Internal Data

Regardless of the type of model you are constructing, some of the data needed for cost modeling can come directly from your company's own information systems and personnel. Enterprise resource planning (ERP), procurement, ABC, and standard cost systems are some of the best resources to collect general ledger information and commodity-level information. Human resource management systems are also excellent sources of information if the project you are modeling has variables surrounding work hours and wages internal to the business. Operations or project personnel in the areas to be modeled should also be engaged in developing the model so that "hidden costs" are able to be identified and incorporated into the

Example 2.7. Cost Model Dashboard Update

The corporate store operations manager and the XYZ Apparel team completed their cost model and gathered all the necessary inputs to feel confident in the results. Based on the decision variable data collected and the team's most realistic scenario about assumption variables, the recommendation to leadership became clear.

INPUTS

Decision Variables

Make vs. Buy	Buy
Packaging	On Hanger
Transportation mode	Ocean

Assumption Variables

		UOM
Labor rate	$12.25	Hour
Lost sales	5%	
Currency exchange (Chinese Yuan to USD)	6.61	Yuan
Interest rate	5.75%	
Import duties (based on packaging—impacts goods classification)	12.50%	
Transportation expenses (based on modal decision)	$2,500	Container
Packaging costs (based on packaging decision)	$1.53	Carton

Dark gray fields vary with decision variables
Light gray fields are user-input variables

OUTPUTS

Store Associates

Labor cost	$ 13,600
Ocean freight	$ 12,500
Truck freight	$ 18,500
Import duties	$ 3,000
Packaging cost	$ 1,675
Hanger cost (domestic)	$ 5,750

TOTAL COST	**$ 55,025**

Supplier

Labor cost	$ 0.06	$ 3,238
Ocean freight	$ 0.30	$ 15,000
Truck freight	$ 0.46	$ 23,000
Import duties	$ 0.08	$ 4,000
Packaging cost	$ 0.08	$ 3,889
Hanger cost (international)	$ 0.08	$ 4,000
Sales gain (measured by gross margin)	35%	$ (13,155)

TOTAL COST	**$ 39,972**

With 50,000 units annually requiring unfolding, hanging, and steaming and an average selling price of $15 per garment, the team determined that the difference in costs was nominal. However, a conservative assumption was made after further discussions with marketing and store operations managers that reallocating the time store associates spent on this activity to more sales-focused customer interaction would cause an increase in sales of at least 5%. When the gross margin dollars of this sales gain are added back into the equation, the case for a switch to the supplier model became more compelling.

model. Cross-functional participation within the enterprise is probably the single biggest contributor to cost model accuracy.

Supplier Provided Data

Supply chain professionals will frequently work with supply organizations to better understand the costs associated with conducting a line of business. If customer-supplier bonds are close, it is not uncommon for suppliers and customers to share information with the intention of reducing overall supply chain costs. In these open-book strategic relationships, information flows more freely, and it is easier to identify specific areas of disproportionate cost. However, the vast majority of customer-supplier relationships are not so strategic in nature, and prying cost information from suppliers can prove particularly difficult. Supply chain professionals faced with this challenge generally collect cost details by making its inclusion mandatory as part of a request for information (RFI) or request for proposal (RFP). Collecting cost information from multiple suppliers can provide current market-based cost information that can be instrumental in evaluating pricing proposals and forecasting future costs. Additionally, supplier site visits and investigating supplier websites and annual reports can provide further insight into supplier costs and influencing factors.

External Data

External (third-party) data sources can be utilized in a number of cost model types, particularly in defining assumption variables. Because assumption variables are tied to uncontrollable external forces, many of the assumption variables, such as currency fluctuations, commodity prices, and interest rates, are tied directly to indices designed to track their change over periods of time. Use of external data in this manner is not uncommon. However, supply chain managers frequently utilize outside data sources in more sophisticated manners to determine what a product or service truly costs the supplier to provide. This cost information is then utilized in a negotiating setting to lower prices based on facts collected. A listing of some of the most prevalently referenced sources of external data are shown in Table 2.2, and several of these will be discussed in more detail in the external cost modeling chapters. Information about how to find and access these sources is contained in appendix A.

Table 2.2. Prevalently Referenced External Data Sources

U.S. publicly available	International publicly available	Subscription required
Economic consensus	World Bank	Hoovers
• 2007 economic census & surveys	NationMaster	Dun & Bradstreet
• Annual survey of manufacturers	UK Office of National Statistics	RMA Annual Statement Studies
Bureau of Labor Statistics	Statistics Norway	Almanac of Business & Industrial Financial Ratios
• producer prices indices	National Bureau of Statistics of China	Industry Norms & Key Business Ratios
• wages by area & occupation	Japan Statistics Bureau & Statistics Center	
• earnings by industry	Australian Bureau of Statistics	
• labor & productivity costs	Eurostat Statistical Office of the European Commission	
• international labor comparisons	Statistics Canada	
• international price indices	Statistics South Africa	
• international productivity	Statistics New Zealand	
IRS tax stats		
Federal Reserve Board		
Bureau of Economic Analysis		
Department of Energy		
Bureau of Transportation Statistics		
Federal Motor Carrier Safety Administration		
EDGAROnline		
Salary.com		
Various trade associations		

CHAPTER 3

Internal Cost Models

Watch the costs and the profits will take care of themselves.

—Andrew Carnegie

An internal cost model is one produced to understand the cost structure of products and services produced within your organization and to aid in decision making. Internal cost models have many uses. Among them are new product and service development, cost reduction, efficiency improvement, production planning, capacity planning, and as components of quality management systems.

All productive organizations have at least some sense of the cost to produce their products and services. Often, though, the cost information is incomplete, inaccurate, or out of date, which brings the principle of "garbage in, garbage out" into play when this cost information is used in decision making. It is important that decisions are made based on complete, accurate, and up-to-date information. Internal cost modeling is a way to assure the completeness and accuracy of cost information.

Internal cost models are most often developed by operations managers, process engineers, quality engineers, supply managers, and cost accountants either individually or in cross-functional teams. Selection of the appropriate type of cost model is important. But most important is assuring that the cost model motivates action. The model by itself does not create improvements in cost, performance, or competitive position. Those improvements result from appropriate actions by management guided by the information the model provides.

External cost models are usually developed at the net profit level, as shown in Figure 3.1, while internal cost models are most frequently developed at the gross profit level. Within an organization, sales, general, and administrative (SG&A) costs and research and development (R&D) costs are not generally allocated to specific products but are deducted

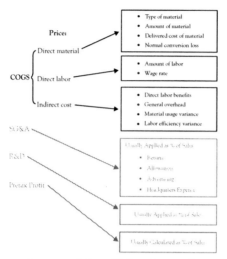

Figure 3.1. General cost model applied to internal cost models.

from total gross profits on the profit and loss (P&L) statement to obtain net profit. When developing external cost models, it is important to include SG&A and R&D costs, where applicable, as well as a reasonable profit in order to determine what a product or service should cost to purchase. When developing internal cost models, the focus is usually more on the production costs specifically associated with the products or services being studied rather than on the final cost burdened with SG&A and R&D. For internal models built to support pricing models, SG&A and R&D costs may be allocated as a percentage, as is usually done when developing external cost models (chapters 5 and 6).

Cost Feasibility Analysis for New Products and Services

A key aspect of new product and service development is the assessment of a feasible price point. A price point target is usually set during the early stages of development. At various points during the development process, it is desirable to construct cost models to determine how close the projected cost is to the target. The objective is to construct the bill of materials (BOM), bill of labor (BOL), and estimated overhead, the sum of which represent the total cost of production of the product or service being designed. The combination of these cost components is often represented in a master file such as the one shown in Example 3.1.

The process of creating an internal cost feasibility model is not unlike that of creating an external projected cost model. The big difference (and advantage) is that in the case of an internal cost feasibility model, the modeler has full access to the cost information already developed in the organization. This can greatly decrease the time requirement for creating the model and increase the model's accuracy. The internal cost model can be as simple or complex as is necessary to answer all the questions it is intended to address. Frequently, a simple cost model is sufficient:

$$\text{total cost} = \text{direct material} + \text{direct labor} + \text{overhead}.$$

Direct material requirements can be determined using the engineering design drawings, specifications, and BOM. Costs for these materials can be determined using existing data if the materials are common to existing products. If the materials are new, costs can be determined using supplier price quotations or catalog prices. Applicable scrap factors should be included in the model. For example, if a component with a circular cross section is stamped from a square blank, there will be unavoidable scrap. This scrap may be minimized by, for example, resizing the blank or using an optimization program designed to maximize the amount of good product obtained from a given blank. Avoidable scrap, such as an allowance for a certain percentage of defective products, should always be included separately so that it is visible and subject to efforts to reduce it.

Direct labor hours can sometimes be determined by combining elements of existing processes to build up a model of the labor required for the new product. If the product is entirely new to the organization, predetermined time standards may be used to develop the direct labor hours required. Using the required labor hours estimate and existing standard labor rate information, an estimate of the direct labor cost can be obtained.

Overhead costs may be estimated in several ways. If the organization applies overhead costs based on direct labor hours, direct labor dollars, or units of production, a first-order estimate can be developed using the existing overhead application factor. If this first-order estimate is insufficient for the purposes for which the model is being developed, the actual overhead to be applied to the new product or service can be built up. The first step in this process is to break the total overhead cost into fixed

and variable components. Fixed costs are constant regardless of the production volume over a relevant range of production. Examples of fixed
overhead costs are general costs for space and utilities, tooling, and production equipment. Variable overhead costs are incurred with each unit
of production. Examples of variable overhead costs are specific costs for
utilities to run production equipment and task lighting at workstations,
in-process inspection and testing, and benefits for direct labor employees.
If no production occurs, all the fixed costs but none of the variable costs
is incurred.

A better estimate of variable overhead cost may be obtained by analyzing the process, determining the actual variable overhead costs incurred
during the study period, and allocating those costs to the units produced
during the study period to obtain the variable overhead cost per unit.
This allocation of specific costs to products or cost centers is the approach
taken by an activity-based costing (ABC) system:

$$\frac{\text{Variable overhead incurred}}{\text{Number of units produced}} = \text{Variable overhead cost per unit.}$$

Example 3.1 illustrates how a simple cost model may be constructed.

The estimates from the cost model of total cost of production can
be compared with target costs established when the development project
was initiated and with target prices to estimate profit margins for the
product or service under development. These comparisons are valuable
in determining design changes that might be needed to bring costs closer
to target, establishing a new target price, or even determining whether it
is feasible to continue the development project. The more accurate the
cost estimates are, the better the decision based on those estimates will be.

Example 3.1. New Product Internal-Projected Cost Model

Our division has been tasked with producing accessory part kits to be included with a new product. The kits consist of two bolts and two nuts packaged in a poly bag. The direct material costs were estimated as shown in Table 3.1 based on catalog costs for the BOM items purchased in bulk quantities.

Table 3.1. Estimated Material Costs for Accessory Kit P/N 007-040

	Part	Unit of measure	Total cost
	01-01 Accessory Kit P/N 007–040	1 kit	
	02-01 2 × 2" Poly Bag P/N S–267	1 each	0.0180
	02-02 Grade 5–5/16"–18–2.5" Hex Bolt P/N B–432	2 each	0.5000
	02-03 Grade 5–5/16"–Hex Nut P/N N–432	2 each	0.0484
	01-01 Total direct material cost		$0.5664

Direct labor cost was estimated using method time measurement (MTM), a predetermined time standard method. MTM uses tables of micromotions with standard time values measured in time measurement units (tmu), which are 10^{-5} hour or 0.036 seconds in duration. The steps involved in using MTM are as follows: (a) define the micromotions (e.g., reach, grasp, move, release) required to complete the job, (b) find the appropriate time using the MTM tables for each micromotion, (c) sum the micromotion times to obtain the synthetic performance normal time for the job, (d) apply the appropriate allowance factor to obtain the synthetic performance standard time for the job, and (e) multiply the standard labor time by the standard labor rate to obtain the synthetic standard direct labor cost.

Table 3.2. MTM* Table for Accessory Kit P/N 007-040

Element	Description	Hand	MTM code	Tmu
1	Reach and grasp poly bag	L	R14B	14.4
			G4A	7.3
2	Move to center of work space	L	M14B	14.6
3	Grasp and open poly bag	L&R	P2S	16.2
4	Reach and grasp 2 bolts	R	R10C	12.9
			G4A	7.3
5	Move and release into poly bag	R	M10A	11.3
			RL1	2.0
6	Reach and grasp 2 nuts	R	R10C	12.9
			G4B	9.1
7	Move and release into poly bag	R	M10A	11.3
			RL1	2.0
8	Grasp and close poly bag	L&R	P2S	16.2
9	Move and release completed kit	L	M12B	13.4
			RL1	2.0
10	Hand to starting position	L	M12A	12.9
	Direct labor synthetic time in tmu			165.8

*The reader is directed to the following resources for detailed information about the use of predetermined time standards: *What Every Engineer Should Know about Manufacturing Cost Estimating* by E. Malstrom, 1981, New York, NY: Marcel Dekker and *Methods, Standards, and Work Design* by B. Niebel and A. Freivalds, 2005, New York, NY: McGraw Hill Higher Education.

Converting tmu into seconds results in 165.8 × 0.036 = 5.9688 seconds or 0.001658 hours for the job. The allowance factor for this job (allowances for basic fatigue, environmental conditions, monotony, etc.) was determined separately as 22% based on job time. This is used to convert the synthetic normal time into standard time for the job by multiplying the synthetic time by the allowance factor: 0.001658 × 1.22 = 0.00202276 hours. The standard wage rate for employees doing this job is $12 per hour, resulting in a standard direct labor cost of $0.02427312 per unit.

Overhead is calculated in this organization as a percentage of direct labor cost. The overhead factor for this department is 150%. The overhead to be allocated to the job is calculated as $0.02427312 × 1.50 = $0.03640968. We may now calculate the projected standard cost to produce the kit using the simple cost model:

$$total\ cost = direct\ material + direct\ labor + overhead$$

$$\$0.6270828 = \$0.5664 + 0.02427312 + 0.03640968.$$

Learning Curve Cost Model

Learning curve cost models focus on the direct labor part of the general cost model. Learning curve cost models recognize that for many labor-intensive processes, the more times the process is repeated, the less time is required per repetition. We experience the learning curve effect whenever we purchase a new electronic device such as a computer, cell phone, or surround sound system. At first we must consult the documentation and experiment in order to make the device perform. We become more comfortable with the device very quickly and over time can make it perform naturally and almost without thinking about it.

The rate of decline in time per repetition is represented by the learning rate, which depicts the logarithmic relationship between the time required for each repetition and production over time. The learning rate is more rapid in the early stages after the start-up of a new process and gradually declines over time. A learning rate of 100% indicates no learning over time, while a learning rate of 90% indicates a 10% reduction in time required per unit for each doubling of the production output. Table 3.3 demonstrates the effect of a 95% learning rate on a process that initially requires 50 hours of direct labor per repetition (unit). As you can see, over time many more repetitions are required in order to obtain smaller and smaller reductions in hours per repetition.

Figure 3.2 graphically depicts the example in Table 3.3 using a 95% learning rate and compares that rate to 90% and 80% learning rates. As you can see, the learning rate curve is initially much steeper for the 80% learning rate than for the 90% and 95% learning rates. So selection of the appropriate learning rate is extremely important.

Table 3.3. Ninety-Five Percent Learning Rate Example

Number of repetitions	Hours per repetition*	Reduction in hours per repetition
1	50.00	–
2	47.50	2.50
4	45.13	2.37
8	42.87	2.26
16	40.73	2.14
32	38.69	2.04
64	36.75	1.94

The values in this column can be calculated using a spreadsheet program such as Excel. To obtain the hours per repetition for two repetitions, type the following into a cell in Excel: =50.95. The result will be displayed as 47.5.

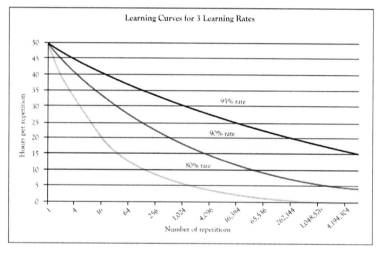

Figure 3.2. Examples of learning curves.

It is possible to calculate the hours per unit for any number of repetitions using the following equation:

$$T_n = T_i \times n^{\ln LP/0.6931472},$$

where T_n is the production time for the nth unit, T_i is the production time for the initial unit, ln is the natural logarithm (base ~2.71828), LP is the learning rate expressed in decimal form, and 0.6931472 is the natural log of 2 (ln 2). Using the equation from the previous example to calculate the

production time for the eighth unit with a 95% learning rate T8 = 50 ×
$8^{\ln 0.95/0.6931472}$, yields a production time for the eighth unit of 42.87 hours.
Natural logarithms can be determined using spreadsheets such as Excel.
Putting =LN(2) into a cell in Excel returns the value of the natural log of
2 =.693147. To program Excel to calculate T8 in this example, type the
following into a cell: =50*8^(LN(0.95)/0.6931472). The result will be
displayed as 42.86875.

While mathematically the rate of reduction in hours per repetition
never reaches zero, practically there are often limits to the reduction in
hours per repetition that may be achieved. This limit must be determined
empirically for each process. For example, using the data in Table 3.3,
there might be machine interfaces, process requirements such as curing
time, or human physical constraints that do not permit the task to be
completed in fewer than 40 hours. In this case the learning curve would
be truncated at 1,600 repetitions and extended as a horizontal line, as
shown in Figure 3.3. The learning rate of 95% would be used for the
first 16 units of production and a learning rate of 100% (no reduction in
hours per repetition) would be used for all remaining production.

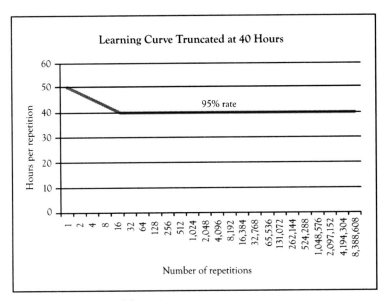

Figure 3.3. Truncated learning curve.

While some learning is almost automatic, the rate may be enhanced by management actions to provide appropriate motivations to improve, implementing improvements to the process, materials and methods, and the amount of training provided to workers. The rate of reduction in time per repetition will be reduced by high employee turnover rates, inadequate training, an organizational culture that does not encourage and support improvement activities, and indifference by management.

Different rates of learning occur for different processes. Learning is usually modest and of short duration for very simple tasks such as packaging operations and more dramatic and of longer duration for more complex tasks such as the assembly of a personal computer. For this reason, learning curves are generally applied to the analysis of more complex tasks. Engineering judgment and experience are used to set a projected learning rate that is then validated using pilot studies or upon the actual start-up of the process.

Learning curve cost models are useful in many ways, including pricing decisions, capacity planning, and scheduling. The cost feasibility analysis is often done for the first unit produced. When initial cost feasibility analysis is combined with learning curve analysis, projections can be made for increases in labor efficiency over time. Prices may be set lower than the initial cost feasibility analysis would indicate when used alone to reflect the expected learning rate and associated cost decrease, thus enabling a greater initial market penetration. When capacity planning and scheduling reflect the learning rate, more realistic plans result.

Learning curve cost models can also be quite useful in purchasing negotiations for new products or with new suppliers of custom products. The objective of the negotiation would be to arrive at a dynamic pricing model that reflects an agreed-on learning rate. That provides the opportunity to share the cost reduction benefits between producer and purchaser and serves as an incentive for the producer to assure that the agreed-on learning rate is achieved. Handled correctly, the use of learning curves can help assure the price competitiveness of the supply chain.

Internal Cost Modeling as an Input to the Pricing Decision

Pricing decisions are generally made based on either a cost or market basis. In market-based pricing, prices are based on competitor pricing for comparable products or services and the organization's marketing strategy. Organizations are often forced into using market-based pricing— particularly for commoditized products and services where competition is fierce. Organizations that wish to sell into these markets must set competitive prices regardless of costs of production in order to achieve market share targets. Cost modeling can be of value in market-based pricing decisions by providing accurate information about the variable and fixed costs of production. A firm may elect to produce a product with a negative profit margin based on total cost if the price is sufficient to cover all variable costs plus make a contribution to fixed costs. If overall production volume in the facility is sufficient to make up the difference in the uncovered portion of fixed costs allocated to the product being priced, the firm may elect to produce the negative gross margin product.

With cost-based pricing, prices are based on production costs plus desired profit. Organizations are generally able to use cost-based pricing for new products, ones that have a significant advantage in the marketplace, or ones for which few competitive alternatives exist.

The modeler should always be explicit about the time frame and any assumptions implicit in the model. Initial cost models are often made based on the cost of the first units produced. This model may be modified to show the expected cost after the production of a specific number of units assuming a certain learning rate, a targeted continuous improvement goal, or expected economies of scale. Where learning rates or continuous improvement goals are considered, it is often best to construct a base model without these improvements and additional models to show the anticipated lower costs associated with achieving the learning rate, continuous improvement target, and economies of scale.

Internal Cost Modeling in Cost Reduction/Continuous Improvement Programs

To be able to improve something, you have to know how to measure it.

—Greg Brue

Cost models for internally produced products and services can be of great value in identifying sources of waste and, in conjunction with traditional lean operations tools such as value stream mapping, can contribute to the improvement of operations. Sometimes just the process of constructing the cost model reveals previously unrecognized cost components that may not be competitive. Internal cost modeling has been used to help organizations as diverse as chemical manufacturers, and airlines and hospitals achieve multimillion-dollar cost savings and performance improvements.[1]

Internal cost models are easier to construct than external cost models primarily because the analyst has readily available access to cost data and to the processes themselves. The information required to construct an internal cost model is contained in the BOM, BOL, and standard cost master files. Standard cost information, including BOM and BOL, is often consolidated into a master file. The job of creating internal cost models is simplified for organizations using ABC. ABC is an overlay to an organization's traditional accounting system that specifically assigns costs to the activities in which they occur.[2] A frequently encountered problem, however, is that the internal cost data are not always accurate or sufficiently complete to support the decision-making process.

Internal Cost Modeling to Support Projects to Increase Efficiency or Reduce Costs

Becoming more lean, increasing efficiency, minimizing bottlenecks, and reducing costs are imperatives for most organizations. Programs such as Six Sigma, lean operations, and just-in-time (JIT) focus on identifying and eliminating, or at least minimizing, sources of waste in a system. Value stream mapping, seven wastes, and 5S are frequently used tools in these programs. Cost modeling can be a valuable addition to this toolbox.

The process of creating an internal cost model to determine how much a product or service should cost to produce is identical to that used to create external cost models of the same type (chapters 5 and 6).

The source information for constructing an internal cost model already exists within most organizations in the form of BOM, BOL, and master files, thus greatly simplifying model building. However, this data, even if accurate, is usually not in the form or level of detail required for cost modeling. The job of a cost modeler is to drill down into the data to create a cost model that accurately portrays the categories of costs and distribution of costs among those categories. This process can turn a standard cost model used for accounting and planning purposes into one that can identify sources of waste and suggest areas for improvement. Example 3.2 is an actual example from one of the author's experiences.

Example 3.2. Internal Cost Modeling for Cost Reduction and Efficiency Improvement

A new general manager was hired in the 1980s to turn around the fortunes of a magnetic media producer. The company had been losing money, and improvements in cost and efficiency were among the keys to returning the company to profitability. One of the first things the new general manager did was to conduct a cost analysis of the leading products produced in the factory. The company used a cost accounting system based on a manufacturing master file—a combination of BOM and BOL. Table 3.4 shows the entry for one of the major sellers produced by the company.

The first cut through the cost analysis identified significant sources of waste. These waste sources consisted of non-value-added activities and scrap factors built into the standard cost.

Further analysis of the subassembly 77–7640 (tape), which is produced in-house, revealed that a 7% scrap factor was included in its factory direct cost (FDC). This adds $14.88 in waste allowed by the standard per 1,000 units of end product resulting in a total waste of $72.37 per 1,000 units or 12.37% of the FDC of the unit.

Examination of the P&L statement showed that the plant was averaging a 0.44% material usage variance (material usage above standard) based on total materials usage and a 23.4% labor efficiency variance (labor usage above standard). This adds an additional $0.196 in material waste and $3.01 in labor waste per 1,000 units resulting in a total waste of $78.58 per 1,000 units or 13.43% of the FDC per unit.

Table 3.4. Sixty-Minute Type II Audio Cassette Tape (per 1,000 Units)

PN/Opn.	Description	Status	Matl.	Labor	O/H	FDC	Standard	UM
04–03	Rework	OP		1.928	6.748	8.676		
77–1112	C–0	RM	152.123			152.123	1.06380	EA
77–2200	Spl. tp.	RM	3.595			3.595	0.00168	RL
77–7640	Tape	SA	134.300	15.300	62.900	212.500	340.0000	FT
05–03	Load	OP		5.192	18.172	23.364		
06–03	Ck. audit	OP		3.461	12.114	15.575		
77–3137	Label	RM	14.310			14.310	2.22200	EA
07–03	Label	OP		5.192	18.172	23.364		
77–3225	Insert	RM	20.620			20.620	1.03100	EA
77–1305	Pl. box	RM	53.025			53.025	1.01000	EA
08–03	Boxing	OP		3.461	12.114	15.575		
77–2058	O/W	RM	10.800			10.800	1.35000	EA
77–2010	Tear stp.	RM	0.068			0.068	0.00003	LB
09–03	O/W	OP		1.731	6.059	7.790		
77–4118	In. Ctn.	RM	13.491			13.491	0.08500	EA
77–2004	Srk. wrp.	RM	0.708			0.708	0.00030	LB
77–4018	Mst. ctn.	RM	1.576			1.576	0.00355	EA
13–03	Pkg.	OP		1.731	6.059	7.790		
FDC			404.616	37.996	142.338	584.950		

Status key: OP = operation, RM = raw material, SA = subassembly.

Table 3.5. Non-value-Added Components in Standard Cost

Waste description	Cost (dollars per 1,000 units)	Percentage of factory direct cost (FDC)
Operation 04–03 (rework) is a non-value-adding activity.	8.67	
Raw material 77–1112 (cassette shell C–0) has a 0.06380-unit (6.38%) scrap factor built in. This implies that the loading operation (05–03) also has a 6.38% scrap factor built in.	9.71 1.49	
Subassembly 77–7640 (tape) has a 50-foot (15%) scrap factor built in.	31.88	
Raw material 77–3137 (label) has a 0.222-unit (11%) scrap factor built in. This implies that the labeling operation (07–03) also has an 11% scrap factor built in.	1.57 2.57	
Raw material 77–3225 (insert) has a 0.031-unit (3.1%) scrap factor built in.	0.64	
Raw material 77–1305 (plastic box) has a 0.010-unit (1%) scrap factor built in. This implies that the boxing operation (08–03) also has a 1% scrap factor built in.	0.53 0.16	
Raw material 77–4118 (inner carton) has a 0.017-unit (2%) scrap factor built in.	0.27	
Total waste cost (dollars per 1,000 units)	57.49	9.8

A similar analysis was conducted for several other high-volume products and the waste amounts were found to be similar to this product. Analysis of all the individual products proved unnecessary since process improvements to reduce waste for one product accrued to all products of this type produced in this facility.

This analysis resulted in engineering projects whose goal was to reduce waste in this product line by 1% of FDC per month over the next 6 months to ultimately cut the waste in half. These projects included the replacement of some equipment that was old, inefficient, difficult to maintain, and generating a disproportionate amount of defective product. Some existing equipment was upgraded with digital controls that allowed for fine tuning of the processes. Manufacturing standing operating procedures (SOP) were reviewed and improved and operators were trained in the new procedures. Sourcing of raw materials was reviewed to assure that all suppliers were providing the best buy combination of quality and price. The result was that the cost reduction goal was achieved in less than 6 months and the process improvements also improved product quality and consistency resulting in increased customer satisfaction. The overall effect on the organization was a return to profitability within 3 months of initiating the improvement projects.

Integration of Multiple Models

While each of the models discussed in this chapter can be used on a stand-alone basis, they are often used in combination. For example, in new product and service development, a learning curve cost model might be developed, followed by a cost feasibility model using labor cost data for a specific point on the learning curve, followed by a breakeven analysis to determine the production volume required to break even at that point.

Each type of model is designed for a specific purpose, so selection of the appropriate combination of models to fit the project requirements is important. Most important, however, is that creating good models does not of itself improve anything. It is the actions by management that the models facilitate that create the improvement. In most cases, cost is usually just one of many factors that are important to the quality of the final decision. Cost models therefore should be viewed as just one input to the decision-making process.

CHAPTER 4

Other Internal Cost Models

There are other types of internal cost models in addition to those discussed in chapter 3 that address the question of what should a product or service cost to produce internally. This chapter discusses four of these models: simple and stepped breakeven point models, make-or-buy decision models, crossover charts, and cost-of-quality models. The output from these models used singly or in combination can provide information that can significantly improve the quality of decisions relating to new product and service introduction, outsourcing, process selection, procurement, and overall cost management.

Breakeven Models

Breakeven cost models focus on the price and cost of goods sold (COGS) portions of the general cost model. A breakeven cost model can be used to determine the relationship between sales volume, expressed as total revenue; fixed costs of production; and variable costs of production. Breakeven models are useful in new product/service development for determining the sales volume necessary to break even, called the breakeven point (BEP), and thus can provide a lower bound on the sales volume necessary for project feasibility. By comparing the calculated breakeven point to market forecasts for sales of new products, an informed decision can be made about the feasibility of the new products from a cost and profit perspective. The pieces of information required to construct a breakeven model are the following:

FC	Total fixed costs associated with production of the product or service Examples: property taxes, equipment costs, certain indirect salaries
VC	Variable cost per unit associated with production of the product or service Examples: direct material, direct labor, variable overhead
R	Revenue per unit

Certain assumptions are implicit in the simple breakeven model.

1. The variable cost per unit is constant regardless of production volume. This ignores such things as economies of scale where unit cost decreases as production volume increases. However, unless the magnitude of economies of scale is very great, the linear assumption will generally yield a good estimate of the breakeven point.
2. Revenue per unit is constant regardless of volume. This ignores such things as quantity discounts and variable pricing plans. If this linear assumption is clearly not valid, the revenue per unit can be calculated as a weighted average of the actual prices that are anticipated to be obtained.
3. Fixed costs are fixed regardless of the volume of production. This is generally valid over a relevant range of volumes usually bounded by the upper limit of current production capacity. If the sales forecast falls within the relevant range, this assumption is satisfied. If the forecast is above the relevant range, an adjustment can be made to the model to reflect the additional fixed cost and perhaps altered variable cost associated with an additional increment in capacity. The adjusted model is referred to as the stepped breakeven model.

Simple Breakeven Model

Figure 4.1 shows a graphical representation of the simple breakeven model. Fixed costs are fixed over the relevant range; total revenue and total cost are represented as linear functions (i.e., revenue and cost per unit are constant). The point at which the total revenue (TR) and total cost (TC) lines intersect is referred to as the breakeven point (BEP), which may be expressed in either units (BEP_U) or revenue dollars ($BEP_\$$). At production volumes (PV) above the BEP, total profit is represented by the vertical difference between the TR and TC lines. At production volumes below the BEP, total loss is represented by the vertical difference between the TR and TC lines.

The graphical BEP model is constructed as follows: Plot the fixed cost as a horizontal line extending from that point on the vertical ($) axis. Select an arbitrary production volume (PV) and calculate the total revenue (TR = R × PV) at that point. Plot that point on the graph and connect it to the origin with a straight line. Select an arbitrary PV and

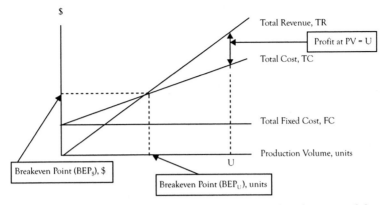

Figure 4.1. Graphical representation of the simple breakeven model.

calculate the total cost (TC = FC + VC × PV) at that point. Plot that point on the graph and connect it to the point where the FC line intersects the vertical axis.

The BEP_U may be calculated by understanding the components of TR and TC. At the BEP, TR and TC are equal:

$$TR = TC$$

TR may be calculated by multiplying the revenue per unit (R) by the production volume (PV). TC may be calculated by adding the total FC to the product of the variable cost per unit (VC) times the production volume (PV). Replacing TR and TC in the previous equation yields the following:

$$R \times PV = FC + VC \times PV.$$

Rearranging the terms yields

$$PV_{BEP} = \frac{FC}{R - VC},$$

where PV_{BEP} represents the BEP—the volume of product at which total revenue equals total cost.

The BEP model may be used to estimate the volume at which a desired profit (DP) is obtained by adding the DP to FC in the previous equation:

$$PV = \frac{FC + DP}{R - VC}$$

In this equation, PV no longer represents the production volume at the BEP but the volume at which the desired profit is obtained. This analysis is often helpful if a new product or service in development has been assigned a target level of profitability. If the model does not show that the target profit can be achieved at forecast volumes of production and target price, the design team can consider other options such as working to reduce product costs through value analysis, adjusting the target price upward, or even terminating the project.

Example 4.1a. Use of the Breakeven Point Cost Model

The following projections apply to a new product under development:

Target price	$550.00
Direct material	$122.00
Direct labor	$27.00
Variable overhead	$166.00
Total variable cost	$315.00
Total fixed overhead to be allocated to product in Year 1	$1,780,000.00*

*This represents the tooling, specialized equipment, and so on associated with the new product.

How many units must be sold in order to break even in Year 1?

$$PV_{BEP} = \frac{FC}{R - VC} = \frac{1,780,000}{550 - 315} = 7,575 \text{ units}$$

The BEP in terms of revenue is 7,575 × 550.00 = $4,166,250.

Example 4.1b. Use of the Breakeven Point Cost Model

Given the market projection for sales during Year 1 is 15,000 units, other information may also be calculated.

Allocate the fixed overhead to Year 1 sales unit: $\frac{1,780,000}{15,000} = 119$ per unit .

Calculate factory direct cost (FDC), gross profit per unit (GPU), and gross margin (GM):

FDC = total variable cost + fixed cost allocation =
$315.00 + $119.00 = $434.00

GPU = revenue per unit − FDC = $550.00 − $434.00 = $116.00

$$GM = \frac{\text{Target price} - \text{FDC}}{\text{Target price}} \times 100 = \frac{550 - 434}{550} = 21.09\% .$$

Calculate projected gross profit (GP) from sales of new product in Year 1:

GP = projected unit sales × GPU = $1,740,000.

Example 4.1c. Use of the Breakeven Point Cost Model

Given that the organization wishes to obtain a Year 1 gross profit of at least $2,000,000, how many units must be sold?

$$PV = \frac{FC + DP}{R - VC} = \frac{1,780,000 + 2,000,000}{550 - 315} = 16,085 \text{ units} .$$

Stepped Breakeven Model

Figure 4.2 shows how the simple BEP model can be modified to account for volumes beyond the relevant range of the simple model's assumptions. This adjustment reflects the increased fixed cost associated with

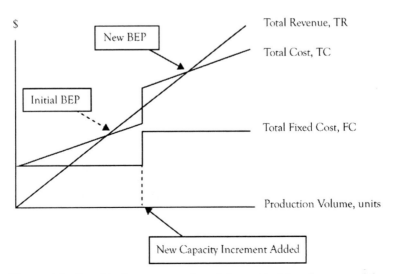

Figure 4.2. Graphical representation of the stepped breakeven model.

adding a new increment of production capacity. The model shows that adding the new capacity increment results in a shift from profitability to loss until the new BEP is reached.

The process for using the stepped breakeven cost model is exactly the same as for using the simple breakeven cost model up to the point where a new capacity increment is added (the upper bound of the relevant range for the simple model). To use the model for production volumes above this upper bound, the process is the same, except the new, higher fixed cost is used as shown in Example 4.2.

Example 4.2. Use of the Stepped Breakeven Point Model

Using the information from Example 4.1 as the initial BEP, calculate the new BEP if a new increment of capacity is to be considered. The new increment of capacity will increase FC to $2,500,000. Revenue/unit and variable cost/unit remain unchanged:

$$PV_{New\ BEP} = \frac{FC}{R - VC} = \frac{2,500,000}{550 - 315} = 10,638 \text{ units.}$$

Sometimes, the VC/unit changes when a new capacity increment is added because, for example, the new equipment may be of a more efficient design. The portion of the product produced on the new equipment will then have a lower VC/unit while the portion of the product produced on the old equipment will remain unchanged. Example 4.3 shows how to calculate the new BEP where the VC/unit changes in this way.

Example 4.3. Stepped Breakeven Point Cost Model With Revised VC/Unit

Using the information from Example 4.2, calculate the new BEP if the VC/unit using the new increment of capacity is $310. The new BEP is the point where the new total revenue equals the new total cost and may be calculated algebraically. The new total revenue may be expressed as

$$TR_{New} = R \times V = \$550 \times PV.$$

The new total cost may be expressed as

$$TC_{New} = FC_{New} + [(VC_{Initial} \times PV_{BEP\ Initial}) + VC_{New}\ (PV_{BEP\ New} - PV_{BEP\ Initial})]$$

$$TC_{New} = 2,500,000 + [(315 \times 7,575) + 310\ (PV_{BEP\ New} - 7,575)]$$

The new BEP ($PV_{BEP\ New}$) is the point where $TR_{New} = TC_{New}$, which, when solved algebraically, results in $PV_{BEP\ New} = 10, 575$ units.

Breakeven models are designed for use in determining the breakeven point for single products. However, by creating a weighted average composite product, multiple products—even an entire facility—can be modeled. This model would be valid so long as the product mix and cost and revenue structure remain unchanged. When product mix, prices, revenues, and/or costs change, a new weighted average BEP model must be constructed.

Make-or-Buy Decision Making

Cost modeling to support make-or-buy decisions focuses on the variable costs of production: direct material, direct labor, and that portion of indirect costs that is variable and that we will refer to as variable overhead. A decision about whether to produce a product or service in-house or to purchase it from a supplier depends on many factors, including cost, quality, availability, and responsiveness. This section addresses the comparison of the cost of in-house production versus the delivered cost of purchasing from a supplier. A key here is to assure that the cost information on which this decision is based is accurate and complete by using cost modeling. In order to be useful, the comparison must explicitly delineate the fixed and variable costs associated with the in-house production of the product:

variable cost of production = DM + DL + variable overhead.

Fixed overhead is that portion of the standard overhead allocated to the product that remains even if production of that product ceases. If production is outsourced, this fixed overhead must be reallocated to the remaining production of other products. One example of fixed overhead is depreciation of the production equipment for outsourced product if the equipment cannot be used for other production or sold at a price at least sufficient to cover its book value. In the case of the sale of the now unnecessary equipment, usually the book value of the equipment will be written off (a one-time charge to the profit and loss [P&L]) instead of continuing the depreciation and offset by the revenue generated by the sale. Another example is the space allocated to the now-outsourced product if it cannot be profitably used for other purposes. Yet another example is the portion of the salaries of indirect employees (e.g., quality manager, production manager, materials handler), which is currently allocated to the now-outsourced product if the employees will be retained after the product is outsourced.

The cost input to the outsourcing decision must compare the outside quotation price, including delivery costs to the variable cost of producing the product in-house. Example 4.4 illustrates a situation encountered by one of the authors involving the cost component of make-or-buy decision making.

Example 4.4. Make-or-Buy Cost Modeling: Trendy Specialty Products Company

The Trendy Specialty Products Company produces a variety of consumer products. One of these products is a promotional flashlight the company assembles from a combination of in-house and purchased components. The materials manager just received an unsolicited quotation from one of the flashlight component suppliers. The quotation was for the complete assembly of the flashlight using existing sources of parts. The price in the quotation was $2.30 per flashlight delivered (FOB destination). The manager compared this quotation with the FDC in the master file of $2.49. He calculated the savings as 2.49 − 2.30 = $0.19 per flashlight times the forecast volume of 8,000,000 flashlights = $1,520,000 for the year. While on his way to present this opportunity to save $1.5 million to the general manager, he chanced upon a consultant employed by the organization to assist in a quality improvement effort. The consultant looked at the numbers and suggested the procurement manager visit with the cost accounting department first and get their assistance in breaking the overhead down into fixed and variable components.

After discussing his analysis with the lead cost accountant, the procurement manager went back to his office. A few hours later, the cost accountant stopped by with her analysis. The fixed portion of the overhead was $0.41 and the variable portion was $0.48. In the ensuing discussion, it was determined that the organization had no immediate productive use for either the space or the equipment they used to assemble flashlights. Because the equipment was of a special design, it was unlikely they could find a ready buyer for it. Only the costs of a dedicated quality inspector, a materials handler, and a supervisor could reasonably be eliminated from the fixed overhead cost. This amounted to about $0.02 per flashlight. The remaining $0.39 of the fixed overhead would have to be reallocated to other products if the flashlight assembly was outsourced. The variable cost of assembling a flashlight was then calculated to be $2.49 - 0.39 = \$2.10$.

The revised analysis compared the variable cost of production to the quotation. Now the comparison showed $2.10 - 2.30 = \$0.20$ loss per flashlight times the forecast volume of 8,000,000 flashlights = $1,600,000 loss for the year if the assembly operation was to be outsourced. The materials manager approached the supplier saying that he would need a delivered price below $2.10 per flashlight in order for the offer to be considered. The supplier was unable to drop the price that much, so the organization continued to produce the flashlights in-house.

As Example 4.4 shows, it can be dangerous to base make-or-buy decisions on models that only use information from the organization's standard cost system, which in this case did not contain sufficient detail to support the decision-making process. Organizations using activity-based costing (ABC) or enterprise resource planning (ERP) systems, which allocate costs more explicitly, have an easier time obtaining the information necessary to construct cost models to aid in make-or-buy decision making for products and the insourcing or outsourcing decision for services.

Process Selection: Crossover Chart

A cost model related to the breakeven model that is useful in process selection and make-or-buy decisions is the crossover chart. This model makes use of the total cost curves constructed in the same manner as the breakeven models to determine the ranges over which two or more options are preferred on the basis of total cost. The information required to construct a crossover chart model are the following:

| FC | Total fixed costs associated with production of the product or service |
| VC | Variable cost per unit associated with purchase or production of the product or service |

The same BEP model assumptions of a linear relationship between VC and production volume and FC being constant over the relevant range apply to the crossover chart model. The TC line is the only line used on the crossover chart and is constructed in the same way as in the BEP model, with its intersection of the vertical axis at the point where the FC line would be drawn. Example 4.5 shows how a crossover chart is constructed and demonstrates its use involving a combination of make-or-buy and process-selection decisions.

Example 4.5. Using the Crossover Chart Cost Model

A product development team is considering three alternative production processes for a new product. Alternative A is to use existing equipment with some minor modifications. Alternative B involves purchasing relatively low-cost new equipment on which to produce the product. Alternative C requires purchasing state-of-the art equipment that is higher in cost than the equipment in Alternative B but has higher production rates. Alternative D involves outsourcing the production of the product. Quotations and cost estimates have been developed for all four alternatives being considered. While cost is only one factor in this decision, it is an important one and will weigh heavily on the final decision.

Alternative	Fixed cost ($)	Total cost per unit ($)
A	30,000	9.50
B	350,000	5.75
C	500,000	3.50
D	100,000*	7.40

*FC is not zero because the supplier requires the buyer to pay for specialized tooling and fixtures.

The team uses this information to construct a crossover chart in order to better compare the alternatives.

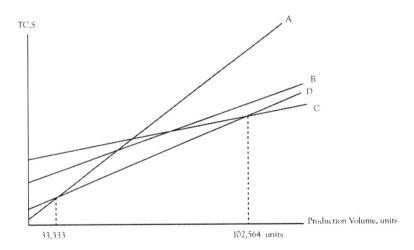

Calculate the production volume for the crossover points where the lowest total cost shifts from one alternative to another. There are two such points on this graph: where A and D cross and where D and C cross.

$$TC_A = TC_D$$
$$FC_A + VC_A \times PV = FC_D + VC_D \times PV$$
$$30,000 + 9.50 \times PV = 100,000 + 7.40 \times PV$$
$$PV = 33,333 \text{ units}$$

$$TC_D = TC_C$$
$$FC_A + VC_D \times PV = FC_C + VC_C \times PV$$
$$100,000 + 7.40 \times = 500,000 + 3.50 \times PV$$
$$PV = 102,564 \text{ units}$$

The crossover chart shows that Alternative A has the lowest total cost for volumes of 1 to 33,333 units, Alternative D has the lowest total costs for volumes of 33,333 to 102,564, and Alternative C has the lowest total cost for volumes in excess of 102,564.

Mathematically, the crossover points are referred to as "points of indifference." That implies that the decision maker is indifferent between the alternatives at the crossover point. Practically, this is rarely the case. At the crossover point, additional information is required in order to make the best decision. For example, at the point where the total cost lines for A and D cross (PV = 33,333 units), the final decision might be based on the forecast volume for the new product. If marketing forecasts initial production volume near the crossover point but substantial growth within a year of introduction, the decision would lean toward Alternative D. If, on the other hand, marketing forecasts initial production volume near the crossover point but declining sales over the ensuing life of the product (think pet rocks of the 1970s), then the decision would lean toward Alternative A.

Cost-of-Quality Models

A quality cost model is a way of showing management that reducing the cost of quality is in fact an opportunity to increase profits without raising sales, buying equipment, or hiring new people.

—Philip Crosby

Cost-of-quality (COQ) models are designed to identify the magnitude and types of expenditures associated with the production of defective products or services and an organization's efforts to prevent and detect those failures. COQ models are frequently used within the quality management system of organizations. Research has shown that quality costs can amount to 10% and in some cases as much as 30%–40% of a product's sales price.[1] In 1996 prior to implementing Six Sigma, General Electric estimated their quality costs at 15% of sales. By 2000 GE estimated they had achieved a $4 billion reduction in the cost of quality through projects directed toward improving processes and products.[2]

Every COQ dollar saved flows to the bottom line with the potential added benefits of possibly increased safety and reliability and increased customer satisfaction due to improved product and service quality. A

COQ model can provide information that can help direct continuous quality improvement activities and document the progress of those initiatives in financial terms. Much of the true cost of poor quality is buried in overhead and variance accounts in an organization's cost accounting system and is not explicitly available to help motivate projects to reduce these costs. One study[3] found that only about one-third of the total costs incurred by an organization due to suppliers' poor quality products are explicit. The other two-thirds of the total cost, including extra inspection, reordering, and extra material handling, are often not explicitly accounted for. COQ provides a significant opportunity for the entire supply chain to identify and reduce the costs associated with poor quality.

As a driver of continuous improvement activities, COQ modeling helped Xerox achieve a $53 million first-year savings,[4] Dow Chemical achieve a $1.5 billion cumulative savings,[5] and CRC Industries to reduce its failure cost by 50% in 4 years from 0.70% to 0.33% of sales.[6] But despite the record of success for cost-of-quality models, studies have shown that only about one-third of business organizations systematically use cost-of-quality modeling.[7]

This section discusses the prevention, appraisal, and failure (PAF) quality cost model, which is the most commonly used form of COQ modeling. A quality cost model takes quality cost information from the organization's traditional accounting system and assigns these costs to four categories: (a) prevention, (b) appraisal, (c) internal failure, and (d) external failure. Prevention costs are incurred to prevent nonconformances from occurring. Examples include design reviews, quality education, quality system audits, and quality administration. Appraisal costs are associated with measurements and inspections to assess conformance to quality standards. Examples include incoming inspections, test equipment and materials, inspection labor, and source inspection. Internal failure costs result from nonconforming products or services detected prior to delivery to customers. Examples include the cost to convene a material review board (MRB), the cost to apply corrective action, the cost to rework nonconforming product, the cost of downgraded end product, the cost of uncontrolled material loss, and the cost of internal design failure. External failure costs result from nonconforming products or services detected after delivery to customers. Examples include returned goods, recall costs, warranty claims, contract penalties, and loss of customer goodwill.[8] Most of these costs are entered into traditional accounting systems but often are aggregated and reported under certain variance and overhead accounts. Creating a COQ model requires identifying the specific quality costs and assigning them to the appropriate COQ category. This task is made easier for firms using ABC or ERP systems, which can be configured to track COQ on a routine basis providing a dynamic model of the firm's expenditures to prevent, detect, and correct quality problems.

Example 4.6 depicts a typical P&L statement for an operating division of a manufacturing company. While some quality costs are evident—for example, rework labor and salary for quality assurance (QA) employees—most are buried within other cost categories. When initially constructing a COQ cost model, additional research is required to drill down into these other categories to find the real quality costs. After these have been identified, standard systems can be introduced to extract these costs and assign them to the appropriate COQ category on a routine basis so that quality costs can be monitored over time. Example 4.7 shows how the quality costs were extracted from the P&L and assigned to the appropriate COQ category.

Example 4.6. Operating Division P&L Statement

			Actual this year ($)	% of sales
Gross revenues			32,356,128	
Less sales returns			1,633,534	5.32
Net revenues			30,722,594	
Cost of goods sold			24,579,864	75.97
Gross profit			6,142,730	18.99
Less sales, general, and administrative (SG&A)			3,636,218	11.84

			Actual this year ($)	% of sales
	Less R&D expense		545,821	1.78
Net profit or loss			1,960,691	6.06
	Direct materials			
		Freight in	663,263	2.16
		Material, price variance	−5,398	−0.02
		Material usage variance	1,489,533	4.85
		Standard material cost	6,675,111	21.73
		Purchase discounts	−12,806	−0.04
		Inventory adjustment	196,020	0.064
	Total materials		9,005,723	29.31
	Direct labor			
		Labor rate variance	291,631	0.95
		Labor efficiency variance	423,876	1.38
		Standard labor cost	2,288,258	7.45
		Downtime	1,137,588	3.70
	Total labor		4,141,353	13.48
	Indirect manufacturing costs			
		Depreciation	2,856,017	9.30
		Safety and insurance	446,501	1.45
		MRO supplies	502,765	1.64
		Occupancy cost	557,652	1.82
		Salary Supervisors	368,519	1.20
		Salary (indirect)	1,232,139	4.01
		Salary engineer	352,040	1.33
		Salary QA	408,366	1.33
		Rework labor	604,327	1.97

				Actual this year ($)	% of sales
			Repairs	305,817	1.00
			Property taxes	789,512	2.57
			Utilities	1,255,437	4.09
			OH variance	69,650	0.23
			FICA, insurance, and benefits	1,684,556	5.21
		Total indirect manu-facturing costs		11,433,308	35.34
Total COGS				24,579,864	75.97

Considerable investigation is usually required in order to properly assign costs from the P&L to the COQ model categories. For example, not all sales returns may be due to quality problems. Some returns might be in conjunction with agreements to accept returns of overstocked or slow-selling merchandise. Only the part of sales returns that is due to defective product should be assigned to the external failure category of the COQ model. In this case, the investigation determined that 40% of the total sales returns was due to defective product (see note 24 in Example 4.7). Example 4.7 shows the assignment of entries from the P&L to the appropriate COQ model categories.

Example 4.7. Assignment of P&L Entries to COQ Categories

Prevention		Appraisal		Internal failure		External failure	
Salary supvervisor[1]	$18,426	Depreciation[6]	$142,801	Material usage variance[13]	$1,489,533	Sales returns[24]	$653,414
Salary indirect[2]	$24,642	MRO supplies[7]	$10,055	Labor efficiency variance[14]	$211,938	Salary supervisor[25]	$18,426
Salary engineer[3]	$52,806	Salary supervisor[8]	$18,426	Downtime[15]	$341,276	Salary indirect[26]	$24,642
Salary quality assurance[4]	$81,673	Salary indirect[9]	$24,642	Occupancy cost[16]	$83,868	Salary engineer[27]	$35,204
FICA, insurance, and benefits[5]	$44,387	Salary engineer[10]	$17,602	Salary supvervisor[17]	$18,426	Salary QA[28]	$61,255
		Salary QA[11]	$183,765	Salary indirect[18]	$123,214	FICA, Ins, and Ben.[29]	$34,132
		FICA, insurance, and benefits[12]	$61,109	Salary engineer[19]	$52,806		
				Salary QA[20]	$81,673		
				Rework labor[21]	$604,327		
				Repairs[22]	$15,291		
				FICA, Ins, and Ben.[23]	$220,112		
Total	$221,934	Total	$458,400	Total	$3,242,464	Total	$827,073

Notes	Notes	Notes	Notes
1 Quality Training—5% of total	6 Test equation—5% of total	13 Usage above standard—100% of total	24 Returns due to quality problems—40% of total
2 Quality training—2% of total	7 QA/QC supplies—2% of total	14 Wasted labor due to quality problems—50% of total	25 Reacting to returns—5% of total
3 Quality training—15% of total	8 Inspection activity—5% of total	15 Downtime due to quality problems—30% of total	26 Reacting to returns—2% of total
4 Quality planning and training—20% of total	9 Inspection activity—2% of total	16 Space charges for rework—15% of total	27 Reacting to returns—10% of total
5 25% of salaries 1–4	10 Inspection activity—5% of total	17 Troubleshooting quality problems—5% of total	28 Reacting to returns—15% of total
	11 Inspection/testing activities—45% of total	18 Troubleshooting quality problems—10% of total	29 25% of salaries 25–28
	12 25% of salaries 8–11	19 Troubleshooting quality problems—15% of total	
		20 Troubleshooting quality problems—5% of total	
		21 Rework of rejects—100%	
		22 Repairs due to quality problems—5% of total	
		23 25% of salaries 17–20	

This COQ model represents a current state model or baseline of the division's quality-related expenditures. Several important pieces of information may be determined from Example 4.7:

- The total cost of quality for this division is estimated by the model at $4,749,871. This is 14.6% of revenues, 19.3% of COGS, and 242% of net profit!
- Just 4.7% of the total COQ expenses are for prevention activities. More than 95% of the expenditures are reactive in nature.

The expenditures on external failure are likely to be understated—perhaps by a considerable amount.[9] Dissatisfied customers who purchase low-cost consumer items are less likely to complain or return the defective items for replacement or refund. They are more likely to simply switch to another brand without telling anyone except neighbors and friends. For more expensive consumer items and for commercial items, dissatisfied customers are more likely to complain and return defective items for repair or replacement. However, in all cases there is usually some loss of customer goodwill, making the customer more open to the possibility of switching brands in the future. Some companies deal with these uncertainties and impossible-to-calculate external failure costs by multiplying the cost of defective product returns by some factor based on marketing research. This provides a better estimate of the true value of external failure costs for the company. One company uses a factor of eight times the actual product return cost because through research they found that only about one in eight dissatisfied customers typically complain or return the defective product. So for every returned item, customer complaint, or warranty claim, this company determined that seven other customers were equally dissatisfied but did not contact the company. The loss of customers, the loss of goodwill, and the effect of dissatisfied customers telling their friends about their bad experience are estimated by multiplying the actual product return cost by the adjustment factor.

Statistics suggest that when customers complain, business owners and managers ought to get excited about it. The complaining customer represents a huge opportunity for more business.

—Zig Ziglar

Presumably, the division in Example 4.7 would not be satisfied with the magnitude of expenditures due to poor quality revealed by the COQ model. What might be some appropriate reactions the division could take to address these costs?

- Analyze the causes of internal and external failures. Initiate programs to address the most frequently occurring ones and set target goals and timetables for improvement.
- Recognize that less than 5% of their COQ expenditures are on prevention activities. Prevention can be viewed as more of an investment than an expenditure. Identify the prevention activities in which to invest (e.g., provide additional operator training, implementing statistical process control [SPC], product or process redesign) in order to prevent the production of defective product. Recognize that the results of these investments will not manifest immediately, thereby resulting in a short-term increase in COQ followed by a long-term reduction as the results of the investments kick in.
- Conduct an internal audit of the division's quality management system. The results of the audit will provide input to management about areas of strength and weakness in the current system. This enables management to make more informed decisions about how to improve.

A quality cost model provides a measurement base for seeing how quality improvement is doing.
—Philip Crosby

By making quality costs visible, a COQ model can provide the impetus for significant improvements. It can also serve as a means for tracking improvement as shown in Example 4.8.

Example 4.8. COQ Distribution Over Time

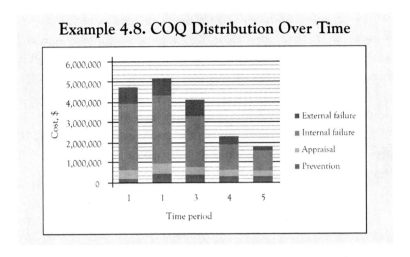

In Example 4.8, Period 1 represents the baseline or current state COQ model for the division. In Period 2, the division has significantly increased investment in prevention activities. The result has been that additional appraisal is needed and internal failure costs increase as more defective products are identified. Overall COQ has increased. In Period 3 the increased investment in prevention activities is beginning to pay off. Appraisal and internal failure costs are down substantially and external failure costs are down slightly as the new product works its way into the downstream supply chain. Periods 4 and 5 show continued improvement in all categories and a substantial overall decrease in total COQ. Note, however, that prevention costs are still higher than the baseline. Investment in prevention activities is not a one-time occurrence. Continued investment is required in order to hold the gains achieved.

Integration of Multiple Models

While each of the internal cost models discussed can be used on a stand-alone basis, they are often used in combination. For example, in new product and service development, a learning curve cost model might be developed, followed by a cost feasibility model using labor cost data for a specific point on the learning curve, followed by a breakeven analysis to determine the production volume required to break even at that point, followed by a crossover model to aid in process selection. All these models used singly or in combination can be extremely useful in providing information vital to decision making in the areas of new product and service development, cost reduction, continuous improvement, efficiency improvement, and quality system assessment and management. Each type of model is designed for a specific purpose, so selection of the appropriate set of models to fit the information requirements is important. And as we have said several times to this point, creating a good model does not of itself improve anything. It is the actions by management that the model facilitates that create the improvement.

CHAPTER 5

External Cost Models for Procured Materials

External cost models are developed by purchasing organizations to gain insight into supplier costs for procured products and services. External cost models are also sometimes referred to as "industry cost models," "projected cost models," or "Should-cost models." A strong understanding of supplier costs assists in ensuring the buying organization obtains goods/services at competitive pricing, future price fluctuations are based on factual cost data, and a mechanism is in place to quantify the cost of design or operational decisions on price.

Though many of the internal cost models discussed in chapters 3 and 4 have been prevalent in the industry for many years, detailed modeling of supplier costs is a more recent phenomenon. Competent organizations are generally more adept at understanding the cost drivers of their internally developed products and services. However, when it comes to developing sources for key products and services to support the core business, far less attention has been paid to supplier cost drivers than to prevalent market conditions, the availability of the product, and the quality of the products and services. With the understanding that supplier cost drivers represent a significant part of the procurement decision, many supply chain and procurement professionals have been utilizing external cost models to improve business intelligence, conduct fact-based negotiations, enhance future price predictability, and facilitate strategic contract formulation for the buying organization.

In chapter 2, we discussed how important it is for the modeler to have a thorough understanding of financial statement analysis. Though that knowledge is necessary for all cost model creation, it is absolutely essential when creating external cost models. Unlike internal cost models, external cost models often require the builder to assess and utilize many different sources of data, meld them together in a meaningful and accurate manner, and draw conclusions relating to potential opportunities. In other words, external cost modeling requires a scientific financial approach to what is an artful exercise in data consolidation, process mapping, and analysis.

All external cost models must start with a backbone of information. Because, as the name implies, external cost models attempt to derive the cost of materials or services produced by suppliers external to the organization, most cost information does not typically reside in the organization's enterprise resource planning (ERP), activity-based costing (ABC), or human resource (HR) systems. Pieces of total supplier cost may be gleaned from those systems, procurement systems, and contracts, but the significant cost gaps that remain must be filled with quality information from other sources. The largest gaps are filled hierarchically by utilizing income statement information from trusted sources. The source for this backbone can vary from supplier 10-K statements, IRS corporate tax tables delineated by industry, economic census data for particular industries, or other credible sources. Several of these sources will be utilized in this chapter when creating a procured materials cost model while also thoughtfully integrating additional information to provide a more accurate view of cost.

Integrating multiple information sources into useful models is typically the responsibility of supply chain and procurement professionals within the business. The ideal time frame to construct a base cost model is prior to entering into a strategic sourcing engagement. This allows for an understanding of the cost structures of the business prior to the solicitation of proposals and the incorporation of cost elements within the questionnaire of any request for information (RFI) or request for proposal (RFP). The cost information received as part of the proposal can be utilized to ensure pricing proposals can be reconciled with cost data, that the cost information is not largely inconsistent with the supplier's peers in the industry, and as the baseline for all future pricing discussions. This allows the buying organization to accurately account for cost elements, such as raw material pricing or labor costs, and how the fluctuations of those elements impact supplier cost over time.

At the highest level, there are two prevalent types of external cost models, those developed to understand cost structures for procured materials and those developed to understand cost structures for procured services. Though both types of models follow the same methodological approach, there are nuances to each, and this chapter focuses on the building and use of procured material cost models.

In Figure 1.1 and in chapter 2, the high-level cost elements utilized for developing cost models were broken out. That base structure will be leveraged in building the procured material cost models outlined in this chapter.

Procured Material Cost Models

Across a wide-ranging number of customers, procured material may have a number of different definitions. For our purposes, we will define procured material as any tangible good that is purchased. This could range from raw materials, such as resin, steel, or commodity chemicals, to large capital equipment, such as gas turbines and ocean vessels. The methodology remains largely the same regardless of the procured material being modeled, only the complexity and depth of the model might differ.

The best way to illustrate the manner in which to build and utilize a procured material cost model is to actually build one. We will use Example 5.1 to walk through how to use external procured material cost modeling to assist a procurement professional make better decisions.

Example 5.1. Corrugate Price Increase

A new category manager of logistics services was hired by a large specialty apparel company, DEF Body, to introduce and utilize world-class strategic sourcing tools and techniques. While conducting a spend analysis of his category early in his tenure, he recognizes the corrugated box product category, with nearly $10 million of spending annually, was escalating at an alarming rate. During the course of his contract analysis, he discovers the category was competitively bid a little more than 3 years previously with the incumbent supplier winning the business and that there are nearly 2 years remaining on the existing nonexclusive agreement. The new category manager finds that the pricing of the specified corrugated boxes was tied entirely (100%)

to a published index from Resource Information Systems, Inc. (RISI) for the two major raw material components (linerboard and medium). This indexing clause seems unusual to the category manager, and he wonders if this might be the cause for the sharp price increases. With an upcoming meeting on this subject already scheduled with members of his leadership team, the category manager seeks to model the supplier costs to arrive at some answers.

The scenario outlined in Example 5.1 is not a unique one. Often supply chain professionals are asked by their supervisors or the business they support to provide assurances that pricing remains competitive. An analysis of the changes in raw material prices does not sufficiently answer the question of whether pricing is competitive. Creating a procured material cost model can provide illumination on whether present pricing remains as cost competitive as when originally contracted. As we develop this case study to create the procured material cost model, we will follow the sequential steps outlined in this chapter.

Creating the Cost Model Backbone

The first step in creating the procured material cost model for corrugated boxes is to find a credible source to utilize as the backbone for the cost model. In this case the corrugated box company is publicly traded, thus their financial data are easily obtainable for review. However, the company is a conglomerate with significant business interests unrelated to corrugated boxes, which can compromise the credibility of the model for the specific industry if used as is. Conducting a search of all the large publicly traded corrugated providers shows that all are conglomerates with significant revenue in other unrelated businesses, so financial information reported publicly would not be specific to the industry segment of interest. Rather than discard this information altogether, the annual reports and 10-Ks are useful in gaining intelligence into trends, forecasts, and general market conditions in the corrugated segment. With specific

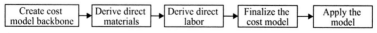

Figure 5.1. Steps in creating a procured material cost model.

industry income statement detail unavailable on 10-K forms, the next best option is to use economic data obtained from census databases for the corrugated industry.

The economic census is a fantastic resource for gaining insight into a particular industry's cost structure. Every 5 years the U.S. Census Bureau conducts extensive surveys of businesses across industries (classified using the North American Industry Classification System [NAICS]) and geographic locations collecting income statements, balance sheets, and other information. Additionally, the U.S. Census Bureau conducts the Annual Survey of Manufacturers that encompasses a smaller sampling of companies for more current detail. The Annual Survey of Manufacturers does not always have the same level of industry specificity (full six-digit NAICS) as the 5-year survey. Unfortunately, that was the case with corrugated boxes, so to ensure we capture the costing information for the specific industry of our interest, we should utilize the 5-year survey information as the backbone on which to build the cost model.

After downloading the industry information from the U.S. Economic Census for NAICS code, 322211-corrugated and solid fiber box manufacturing, a decision needs to be made about whether to utilize only the census data for the backbone or to integrate it with another information source. This is where a strong understanding of income statements and balance sheets comes into play. If the decision is to utilize the census data alone, the modeler must have a strong grasp of which cost lines represented in the data are balance sheet items and which are income statement items. Mischaracterization of those cost lines can distort the output of the model, so as a sanity check it is highly recommended to reference at least one additional secondary source. Some of the more common secondary sources the modeler can reference are IRS tax statistics, *RMA Annual Statement Studies, Dun & Bradstreet's Industry Norms & Key Business Ratios*, or the *Almanac of Business and Industrial Financial Ratios*. Of those references, the IRS tax statistics are available online and free of charge, whereas the other publications require a subscription or trip to your local library to access.

To make the decision of whether to solely utilize the census data, the modeler should consider the age of the information gathered. The census data in this example was obtained from a survey in 2002, and the cost modeler is trying to model the costs for running this business in the 2005–2006 time frame. Certain information from the economic census must be utilized as no other detailed source exists. The specific direct materials and the direct labor components are two pieces of information that are best acquired from the economic census. Overhead or indirect cost is not a figure that can be derived from the economic census data, which makes gross profit incalculable; however, you can lump all the remaining expense items; sales, general, and administrative (SG&A) costs; and other expenses together to derive net profit for the census year.

Another method that may be utilized to bring expenses data up-to-date and to have a more clear understanding of cost of goods sold (COGS) and gross profit is to utilize additional data sources. Several secondary sources are available, but one of the best and most current is the Risk Management Association's *Annual Statement Studies*. This source is updated annually through the membership of thousands of financial institutions and is broken out by NAICS codes, similar to the economic census. From this publication gross profit, operating expenses, nonoperating expenses, and net profit are provided as a percentage of revenue. Example 5.2 illustrates how this information is merged to create the procured materials cost model backbone.

Example 5.2. The Backbone Cost Model

All economic census dollar figures are represented in thousands of dollars.

Backbone Model

Backbone Model					
Revenue	100.00%	←	Total Value of Shipment	$29,514,919	100%
Direct Material	57.91%	←	Materials, Parts, Containers, Packaging, Etc, Used	$17,092,335	57.91%
Direct Labor	9.39%	←	Production Worer Wages	$ 2,770,299	9.39%
Overhead			Annual Payroll minus Production Worker Wages	$ 1,861,555	6.3?%
Operating Expenses			Total Fringe Benefits	$ 1,154,695	3.91%
All Other Expenses			Resales	$ 849,860	2.88%
Net Profit Before Taxes			Cost of purchased fuels	$ 174,234	0.59%
			Purchased electricity	$ 254,680	0.89%
			Contract Work	$ 134,319	0.46%
			Total depreciation	$ 850,911	2.88%
			Total rents	$ 447,508	1.52%
			Total other expenses	$ 1,555,213	5.27%
			Rpr svcs bldgs/mach	$ 303,119	1.03%
			Communivation services	$ 54,294	0.18%
			Legal services	$ 16,559	0.06%
			Actg, aud & bkpg svcs	$ 17,472	0.06%
			Adver & promo svcs	$ 66,007	0.22%
			Comp hdware/purch s/s	$ 27,755	0.09%
			Refuse rem svcs	$ 22,227	0.08%
			Mgmt & admin svcs	$ 26,239	0.09%
			Taxes & license fees	$ 142,168	0.48%
			All other expenses	$ 879,35?	2.98%
			Net Profit Before Taxes	$ 814,098	2.7?%

Revenue, direct material, and direct labor are utilized from the economic census. If the modeler elected to utilize solely the economic census for formulating the backbone of the model, the other income statement fields are grayed and crossed out to indicate lack of use in the example.

Backbone Model			2006–2007 Annual Statement Studies	
Revenue	100.00%		Net Sales	100.00%
Direct Model	57.91%			
Direct Labor	9.39%	74.40%		
Overhead	7.10%		Gross Profit	25.60%
SG&A	23.20%		Operating Expenses	22.10%
			All Other Expenses	1.10%
Net Profit Before Taxes	2.40%		Net Profit Before Taxes	2.40%

Operating expenses and all other expenses are equivalent to the SG&A expenses in our cost model structure and are combined for the backbone model. Net profit before taxes is directly transferable to the backbone model from the economic census data; however, some calculation is required to translate gross profit percentage from the RMA's *Annual Statement Studies* publication into an overhead value in the backbone model. As discussed in chapter 1, COGS = direct material + direct labor + overhead. Because direct labor and direct material are "knowns" from the economic census data, the value for overhead can be calculated utilizing simple algebra

$$Revenue - Gross\ Profit = COGS.$$

First we need to translate gross profit of 25.60% from *RMA's Annual Statement Studies* to COGS. To do this we follow the previous formula to get the following results:

$$100.00\% - 25.60\% = 74.40\%$$

Now that COGS is known to be 74.40%, we can solve for the value of overhead following simple algebraic principles:

$$COGS = Direct\ Material + Direct\ Labor + Overhead$$

COGS represented in algebraic form for this example follows, where "X" is the unknown value of overhead:

$$74.40\% = 57.91\% + 9.39\% + X$$

In order to solve for overhead, the equation needs to be rebalanced:

–Overhead = –COGS + Direct Material + Direct Labor

Then plug-in the numeric values and solve for "X."

–Overhead = –COGS + Direct Material + Direct Labor

$$-X = -74.40\% + 57.91\% + 9/39\%$$

$$-X = -7.10\%$$

$$X = 7.10\%$$

Inserting the overhead value into the backbone model will yield the following high-level results for the backbone of the cost model.

	Revenue	100.00%
COGS	Direct material	57.91%
	Direct labor	9.39%
	Overhead	7.10%
	SG&A	23.20%
	Net profit before taxes	2.40%

(Note: COGS total shown as 74.40%)

The backbone of the model is sound, but the direct material and direct labor components are dated figures compared to the information obtained from the *RMA Annual Statement Studies*. Although updating these figures will have no impact on the COGS components as a whole, since that is current information from the *RMA Annual Statement Studies*, it will provide valuable insight into the impacts of each on total cost of product. Remember, in this instance 100% of the buying company's price is determined by the fluctuation in linerboard and medium, so understanding the material cost component is of large importance. In order to bring those values current, the combination of economic census data, Bureau of Labor Statistics data, and a third-party trade group can be utilized.

Derive Direct Material Costs

The economic census provides a report by a manufacturing sector called "Materials Consumed by Kind by Industry." This report contains the dollar values of basic materials consumed in performing a particular business. For our example, Figure 5.2 illustrates the data available from the economic census.

In procured material cost modeling, the information from the economic census is extremely important in order to be able to accurately extrapolate present-day costs. In this case there are eight components (individual material/fuel codes) of cost for corrugated and solid fiber box manufacturing. Since the material/fuel code column represents 2002 costs, a method is needed to extrapolate these costs to the present day. One manner in which these materials can be brought to current-day costs is through the use of the Producer Price Index (PPI), available through the Bureau of Labor Statistics (BLS). All the material/fuel codes beginning with the number "3" relate to NAICS industry codes that the PPI reports on monthly. For the last two material/fuel groups, the modeler has to use personal discretion when extrapolating. It should be noted that the modeler has the option of choosing PPI industry data or PPI commodity data. The industry data series is tied to NAICS code industry of origin and thus is easy to extrapolate to the material/fuel code provided in the economic census data. The commodity data series is tied to the end-use or material composition of the product produced, but the coding is not tied to the origin industry or NAICS system.

Data presented in the PPI is searchable by NAICS industry code or key word. In Figure 5.3 an example of the PPI data for paper and paperboard is provided for one of the material/fuel codes of interest in creating the corrugated box procured material cost model.

The data represented in Figure 5.3 must be collected for each of the material/fuel codes for the category being cost modeled. Though the material/fuel code provides some directional guidance in regard to

Material/Fuel code	Meaning of Material/Fuel code	Delivered cost ($1,000)
900001	Total materials	17,068,741
32210005	Paper and paperboard (excluding boxes and containers)	13,351,764
32610021	Fabricated plastics products (closures, ends, film, etc.)	117,036
33120016	Steel sheet and strip (including tinplate)	12,427
33131503	Aluminum sheet, plate, and foil	D
33211500	Metal closures and crowns for containers	D
32410009	Petroleum wax	76,296
32552002	Glues and adhesives	276,984
32591003	Printing inks	140,466
970099	All other materials/components/parts/containers/supplies	1,240,975
971000	Materials, ingredients, containers, and supplies, nsk	1,844,160

Figure 5.2. NAICS 322211-corrugated and solid fiber box manufacturing.[1]

Year	Jan	Feb	Mar	Apr	May	Jun	Jul	Aug	Sep	Oct	Nov	Dec	Annual
2000	177.5	178.0	189.8	191.9	196.3	196.2	196.9	197.6	196.6	196.1	195.9	195.6	192.4
2001	195.5	192.3	191.8	191.0	189.5	187.8	187.6	185.0	183.9	181.7	181.4	181.6	187.4
2002	179.4	179.2	177.7	178.0	176.1	176.1	177.4	181.7	182.3	182.7	183.0	182.1	179.7
2003	182.4	183.0	180.4	180.3	180.4	180.1	179.1	182.0	179.7	179.0	178.9	179.0	180.4
2004	176.7	176.4	176.6	182.5	185.0	190.0	196.2	198.8	199.1	199.7	200.3	200.0	190.1
2005	200.2	200.5	200.6	201.3	201.6	197.2	195.8	188.7	188.5	189.1	196.0	195.4	196.2
2006	197.2	205.5	205.0	205.1	216.0	216.9	217.4	217.8	218.1	218.6	219.4	218.5	213.0
2007	219.1	219.6	219.7	221.2	221.0	221.3	221.5	221.7	226.7	233.0	233.5	233.9	224.4
2008	234.2	234.3	234.4	234.4	235.3	237.0	253.0	254.6	255.1	252.6	252.2	242.6	
2009	247.4	244.2	238.9	233.8	228.6	226.5	226.5	227.4	228.3	224.2	224.4	222.9	231.1
2010	222.9	238.8	239.8	242.2	258.4	258.4	259.3	259.4	271.0	261.3	262.7		

Figure 5.3 PPI data paper and paperboard.

the best PPI industry data series to choose, the modeler has to utilize knowledge of the category to select the "best fit" for the category being modeled. In Figure 5.4, the PPI series ID PCU322130332130 relates directly to NAICS code 322130, paperboard mills. The material/fuel code from the economic census was represented as 32210005. NAICS codes are only six digits in length, so the economic census number of 32210005 should be shortened to 322100; however, two zeros at the end of the six digit NAICS string indicates that only a four-digit level of detail is provided from the economic census. So the modeler must begin with the first four digits from the economic census and then decide which full six-digit NAICS code best fits what the cost model is to represent.

Once all the information is collected for each of the material/fuel codes, the percentage change from the period the economic census data was collected to the present day must be determined. To calculate the percentage change for each material/fuel code PPI series, the annual values highlighted in Figure 5.4 are utilized via the following formula:

$$\frac{2006 \text{ annualized value} - 2002 \text{ annualized value}}{2002 \text{ annualized value}} = \text{percentage change}$$

$$\frac{213.0 - 179.7}{179.7} = 18.53\%.$$

For the last two material/fuel codes from the economic census data, no single PPI industry series will provide time series differences, so the modeler must choose a method. One approach that will be utilized here is to assume the change mimics Consumer Price Index (CPI) Inflation. The CPI is not as applicable as the PPI for commercial products but

Material/Fuel code	Meaning of Material /Fuel code	Delivered cost ($1,000)	PPT Series ID (Industry Data)	2006 Escalator Multiplier	Escalated Material	Total Mat'l Increase %
900001	Total materials	17,068,741	N/A	N/A	20,017,808	17.28%
32210005	Paper and paperboard (excluding boxes and containers)	13,351,764	PCU322130322130	1.185	15,825,964	
32610021	Fabricated plastics products (closures, ends, film, etc.)	117,036	PCU326112236112	1.110	129,910	
33120016	Steel sheet and strip (including tinplate)	12,427	PCU331221331221 1	1.393	17,313	
33131503	Aluminum sheet, plate, and foil	D	N/A	N/A		
33211500	Metal closures and crowns for containers	D	N/A	N/A		
32410009	Petroleum wax	76,296	PCU324191324191	1.534	117,015	
32552002	Glues and adhesives	276,984	PCU325520325520	1.177	326,090	
32591003	Printing inks	140,466	PCU325910325910	1.041	146,166	
970099	All other materials/components/parts/ containers/supplies	1,240,975	CPI Inflation Calculator	1.120	1,389,892	
971000	Materials, ingredients, containers, and supplies, nsk	1,844,160	CPI Inflation Calculator	1.120	2,065,459	

Figure 5.4. Extrapolated material costs.

often is the best approximation for when better data is unavailable. The CPI Inflation Calculator is available from the BLS and allows for the calculation of a dollar value in a baseline year, 2002 in our case, to a subsequent year, 2006 for this example. The inflation rate between 2002 and 2006 is represented at 12%, and that value is utilized for those mixed materials.

Once all the material prices are extrapolated to the present day, 2006 for this example, the total material cost differences between those years can be determined. Figure 5.4 provides an illustration of all material costs extrapolated.

As Figure 5.4 indicates, material costs for the products produced in the corrugated manufacturing industry increased by 17.28% from 2002 to 2007. A decision needs to be made here about whether to utilize this information from the PPI and CPI solely or to consult an additional source for particular materials. Because paper and paperboard constitutes greater than 78% of the total material cost for manufacturing a corrugated box, the accuracy of that raw material component in particular is crucial to the integrity of the cost model. If a trusted source with more specificity is available in place of the more generic PPI index in this instance, then the degree of change from that source can be used in place of the PPI data. Example 5.3 allows us to continue following the category manager in his analysis of his category and construction of this cost model.

Example 5.3. Extrapolate Material Pricing to Present-day

The category manager for logistics services now has constructed his backbone cost model and extrapolated the costs from 2002 to the current year (2006) using the economic census data adjusted utilizing PPI and CPI data. As he reviews the raw materials with the most impact on cost, he realizes that paper and paperboard constitute greater than 78% of the material costs to manufacture the product in 2002. He then calculates the cost impact of paper and paperboard materials on the manufacturing of corrugated boxes.

Raw materials × Paper & paperboard % =	Percentage impact of paper & paperboard on manufacturing cost
57.91% × 78.22% =	45.30%

The results of this calculation and the escalation of costs for paper and paperboard products since the contract was executed validates his belief that tying price 100% to the major raw materials (linerboard and medium) is not the best method to ensure sustainable price competitiveness. His tentative conclusion at this point in the analysis is that the contract price should be tied to 45.30% of the materials fluctuations rather than 100%.

To further ensure that his model around material costs is accurate, the category manager compares the percentage increase of the PPI paper and paperboard products to the contractually stipulated index, RISI Pulp and Paper.

He discovered that prices from 2002 to 2003 remained relatively stable, but beginning in early 2004, a large increase in material costs was clearly evident in both indices. The large differences the category manager is seeing between the PPI data and RISI Pulp and Paper raises a further question in his mind as to which index more accurately reflects actual cost fluctuations in the marketplace. With further research, he decides the RISI index is the superior benchmark to utilize as it is a trusted source and provides specific linerboard and medium raw materials price fluctuation data. With DEF Body having pricing

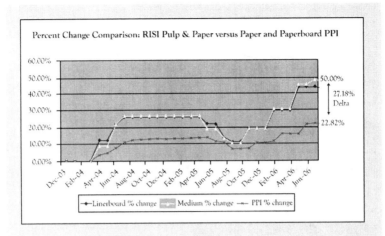

Percent Change Comparison: RISI Pulp & Paper versus Paper and Paperboard PPI

tied 100% to the linerboard and medium costs, he knows the nearly 50% increase in pricing his company has experienced since contract execution is excessive based on his preliminary analysis of the impact of raw materials on manufacturing cost. However, he knows he needs to bring all cost elements from the economic census current (from 2002 to 2006) in order to fully understand the delta between supplier costs and DEF Body's pricing since the bid.

Now that the category manager for logistics services has decided upon a different index, replacement of the PPI index information for paper and paperboard with the RISI index information for linerboard and medium is necessary. The category manager had learned from published information that the typical mixture between linerboard and medium is 75% linerboard and 25% medium, and this also corresponded to how the contract calculated price was adjusted for fluctuations in those two areas. The next step is to apply that percentage to his material costs table and update the escalator multiplier based on the RISI data. As he expected this exercise shows a marked increase in total material costs (39%) since 2002, as illustrated in Figure 5.5.

These new calculated figures will enhance the accuracy of the COGS section of the backbone cost model and provide necessary intelligence to how commodity price fluctuations should impact pricing in the future. After the direct labor component is extrapolated to the present day, the

Material/Fuel code	Meaning of Material/Fuel code	Delivered cost ($1,000)	PPT Series ID (Industry Data)	2006 Escalator Multiplier	Escalated Material	Total Mat'l Increase %
900001	Total materials	17,068,741	N/A	N/A	23,725,809	39.00%
32210005	Paper and paperboard (excluding boxes and containers)	13,351,764				
32210005	Paper and paperboard (excluding boxes and containers)	10,013,823	RISI Linerboard	1.451	14,527,053	
32210005	Paper and paperboard (excluding boxes and containers)	3,337,941	RISI Medium	1.500	5,006,912	
32610021	Fabricated plastics products (closures, ends, film, etc.)	117,036	PCU326112236112	1.110	129,910	
33120016	Steel sheet and strip (including tinplate)	12,427	PCU3312213312211	1.393	17,313	
33131503	Aluminum sheet, plate, and foil	D	N/A	N/A		
33211500	Metal closures and crowns for containers	D	N/A	N/A		
32410009	Petroleum wax	76,296	PCU324191324191	1.534	117,015	
32552002	Glues and adhesives	276,984	PCU325520325520	1.177	326,090	
32591003	Printing inks	140,466	PCU325910325910	1.041	146,166	
970099	All other materials/components/parts/containers/supplies	1,240,975	CPI Inflation Calculator	1.120	1,389,892	
971000	Materials, ingredients, containers, and supplies, nsk	1,844,160	CPI Inflation Calculator	1.120	2,065,459	

Figure 5.5. Escalated material costs.

method to revise the backbone cost model with the updated information will be shared later in this chapter.

Derive Direct Labor Costs

Now that all the materials have been extrapolated to the present day in the cost model, the direct labor component of the model needs to be updated to complete the updated procured materials industry cost model. The primary source of the information will originate from the BLS Occupational Employment and Wage Estimates; however, the economic census provides a needed check point to mitigate any faulty assumptions.

The BLS Occupational Employment and Wage Estimates is a powerful resource for understanding labor costs in any industry represented by NAICS codes. This information is published at least once annually and provides occupational data by job classification with additional details for each classification such as total employees, hourly wages, annual wages, and wages by percentile. To understand the differences from the baseline year of 2002 to present-day 2006 (in the example), the annual figures for both years must be downloaded and analyzed.

The BLS represents the data by industry by NAICS code but never in the full six-digit NAICS code. However, between the four-digit and five-digit NAICS codes, it does provide sufficient data to understand the wage trends in a particular industry. For the corrugated box cost model, the four-digit NAICS code 322100 details are utilized to understand labor and wage trends. Figure 5.6 provides a representation of some of the figures available from the BLS Occupational Employment and Wage Estimates.

Figure 5.6 illustrates a sampling of the labor classifications available, but the classifications of primary interest in cost modeling are those attributable to direct labor. Understanding what labor classifications comprise direct labor is not difficult to discern. The Standard Occupational Codes (OCC) utilized by the BLS are provided at both a detailed and high level. The simplest manner to determine the direct labor component is to filter the OCC Code column for codes beginning with "49" and "51." OCC Codes that begin with "49" are all the installation, maintenance, and repair occupations, while "51" are all the production occupations for the industry and equate roughly to the direct labor component being modeled. In some instances you may selectively choose the occupations within the industry for use in the direct labor component, but whichever method is chosen should have a cross-check with the economic census data. Referring back to the economic census data, the production worker's wages constituted 60.37% of the total wages for the industry. When reviewing the 2002 BLS occupational data and narrowing labor based on the OCC codes that begin with "49" and "51," the labor classifications in the OCC codes comprises 59.97% of the wages for the industry. With these figures being this close, confidence is gained as to the integrity between the two sets of data, and it provides a good audit point for ensuring the accuracy of the model. See Figure 5.7 for further details on these calculations.

Once there is confidence that the direct labor components have been identified, fluctuations between 2002 and the present day (2006

OCC Code	OCC Title	Total Emp's	Percent Total	Annual Mean	Annual 25th &tile	Annual Median	Annual 75th %tile
00-0000	Industry Total	161,030	100.00	43,110	30,970	39,960	51,680
11-0000	Management Occupations	5,950	3.69	92,460	66,940	87,390	111,790
11-1011	Chief Executives	150	0.09	166,070	115,450		
11-1021	General and Operations Managers	1,000	0.62	114,110	82,820	106,840	138,630
11-2021	Advertising and Promotions Managers	30	0.02	100,890	66,540	113,370	143,410
11-2021	Marketing Managers	100	0.06	110,970	78,950	111,060	140,300
11-2022	Sales Managers	320	0.20	98,120	71,170	91,980	116,300
11-2031	Public Relations Managers	30	0.02	70,810	49,330	71,060	91,740
11-3011	Administrative Services Managers	200	0.12	91,460	59,770	85,270	121,610

Figure 5.6. BLS wage data by industry.

2002 BLS Occupational Employment and Wage Estimates Calculations:

OCC Code	OCC Category Title	Total Emp's		Annual Mean Wage		Total Payroll
00-0000	Industry Total	161,030	×	43,110	=	6,942,003,300
49-0000	Installation, Maintenance, and Repair Occupations	22,940	×	47,170	=	1,0821,079,800
51-0000	Production Occupations	79,950	×	38,540	=	3,081,273,000
	Total Direct Labor					4,163,352,800

Total Direct Labor / Industry Total = Percent of Total Labor

4,163,352,800 / 6,942,003,300 = 59.97%

2002 Economic Census Calculations:

Production workers, nonleased / Annual payroll = Percent of Total
employees wages (1,000)   (1,000)   Labor

2,817,454 / 4,667,010 = 60.37%

Figure 5.7. Validated wage data.

in this example) need to be calculated and compared for updating the cost model. Were we to have identified direct labor by occupational title, we would need to track fluctuations across each occupational title; however, since it was decided that the major OCC categories of production and installation, maintenance, and repair occupations were sufficient, a comparison of total wages for those categories across years will provide the needed information. Figure 5.8 illustrates the comparison and wage fluctuation calculation.

		2006		2002		
OCC Code	OCC Category Title	Annual Mean Wage		Annual Mean Wage	=	Annual Mean Wage Increase
49-0000	Installation, maintenance, and repair occupations	$51,130	−	$47,170	=	$3,960
51-0000	Production occupations	$42,210	−	$38,540	=	$3,670

The actual increase needs to be equated to a percentage increase for the baseline year of 2002.

OCC Category Title	Annual Mean Wage Increase	÷	2002 Annual Mean Wage	=	Percentage Wage Increase
Installation, maintenance, and repair occupations	$3,960	÷	$47,170	=	8.40%
Production occupations	$3,670	÷	$38,540	=	9.52%

Those increases by occupational category then need to be applied to direct labor components. Based on the dollars represented in Figure 5.7, the percentage impact to direct labor can be calculated.

	2002 Direct Labor		Wage Fluctuation Multiplier		2006 Direct Labor
Installation, maintenance, and repair occupations	$1,082,079,800	×	108.40%	=	$1,172,992,200
Production occupations	$3,081,273,000	×	109.52%	=	$3,374,689,500
Total Direct Labor	$4,163,352,800				$4,547,611,700

The total increase in direct labor is 9.3% from 2002 to 2006.

Figure 5.8. Wage comparison and fluctuation calculation.

Finalize the Cost Model

All the steps have now been completed to extrapolate costs for direct materials and direct labor to bring the costs to the present day (2006) from the base year of 2002. The final step is to apply the updated analysis to the backbone cost model to have a more accurate representation of the industry.

When viewing the updated cost model from 2006 compared to 2002, the main item that really stands out is the impact of direct materials on the overall cost structure and the revenue stream for the industry. As one would expect, as raw material pricing increases dramatically, so must pricing to ensure costs are met and expected margins are realized. With the completed backbone model in hand, the category manager for logistics services now needs to integrate information specific to his company's corrugated boxes into the model.

Apply the Cost Model

The completion of the backbone cost model is a big step to begin developing a strategy to reduce cost, but by applying the model to the business's specific product provides greater leverage. This process begins with identifying a point in time where pricing was competitive. For the purposes of this example, the competitive point in time was December 2002, when a bid event was completed.

Linerboard and medium play the largest single role in the pricing of corrugate, so that is a good place to begin the analysis. In December 2002 the price per carton was $0.478. Since that period of time, the pricing had risen by 46.24% to $0.699/carton in 2006. Remember that linerboard constitutes 75% of the raw material cost and medium constitutes 25%, as stipulated in the contract. Applying those percentages to the price increases in linerboard and medium over that same time period validates that the rate increase is applied according to the terms of the contract.

When comparing the backbone cost model from 2002 to 2006, the only areas of significant difference are in direct material and direct labor. As calculated in Figure 5.9, the cost of materials and labor (in thousands) increased $6,921,709. That increase was then added to the 2002 U.S.

Direct material and direct labor costs must be multiplied by the inflation multiplier to extrapolate to present-day (2006) costs.

	Fluctuation multiplier		2002 Costs		Extrapolated 2006 costs	Direct material increase
Direct material	1.3900	×	17,092,335	=	23,758,348	
Direct labor	1.0923	×	2,770,299	=	3,025,998	
			19,862,634		26,784,343	6,921,709

Once the direct material and direct labor costs are known, the difference of those costs from 2002 must be added to the revenue for the inustry.

2002 Revenue		2006 Increase		2006 Revenue
29,514,919	+	6,921,709	=	36,436,628

With the new revenue extrapolated, now the direct materials, direct labor must be re-calculated as a percentage of revenue to complete the finalized model.

Backbone Model

		Revenue	36,436,628	
COGS	74.40%	Direct material	23,758,346	65.20%
		Direct labor	3,025,998	8.30%
		Overhead		
		SG&A	8,453,298	23.20%
		Net profit before taxes	874,479	2.40%

Note that the percentage of COGS, SG&A and net profit before taxes remain unchanged as they are direct from RMA Annual Statement Studies for 2006. Overhead, however, was a calculated field based on imprecise data from the 2002 Economic Census integrated with the 2006 RMA Annual Statement Studies. Since the COGS figure for 2006 is a "known" from that publication, the overhead percentage needs to also be re-calculated.

$$-\text{Overhead} = -\text{COGS} + \text{Direct material} + \text{Direct labor}$$

$$-X = -0.74 + 65.20\% + 8.30\%$$
$$-X = -0.89\%$$
$$X = 0.89\%$$

With the last unknown of overhead now calculated, the 2006 cost model for corrugated manufacturing looks like the below.

Backbone Model

		Revenue	36,436,628	100.00%
COGS	74.40%	Direct material	23,758,346	65.20%
		Direct labor	3,025,998	8.30%
		Overhead	324,508	0.89%
		Operating expenses	8,052,495	22.10%
		All other expenses	400,803	1.10%
		Net profit before taxes	874,479	2.40%

Figure 5.9. Updated cost model.

Economic Census revenue figure to derive a 2006 revenue figure. When dividing the economic census revenue reported by the cost materials and labor increased, the cost justified price increase can be calculated.

$$29,514,919 \div 6,921,709 = 23.45\%$$

An increase of 23.45% since 2002 can be justified based on the updated model.

Example 5.4 illustrates how the category manager for logistics services utilizes this applied cost model information to derive value for his organization.

Example 5.4. Using the Model to Derive Value

The category manager is ready to present his findings and recommendations for the strategic next steps to his leadership team. In the meeting with his director and the logistics leadership team, he shares the quick ascent in corrugated pricing versus what his analysis shows is indicative of real cost increases. Further, he displays a chart to leadership that quantifies the magnitude of the annual opportunity in this space.

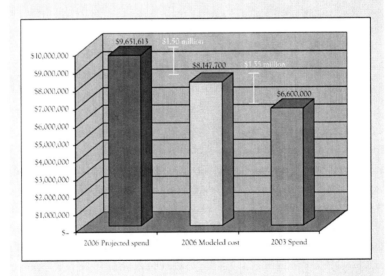

The category manager for logistics services explains to the leadership team that though there are definitive market pressures that are pressing their prices to historic highs, the market pressures alone are not responsible for the inflated prices DEF Body is experiencing. A faulty pricing model combined with the skyrocketing costs in linerboard and medium have made DEF Body's once competitive price evaporate into a margin bonanza for the corrugate supplier.

In discussing strategic next steps, he recommends that the initial approach be a negotiation with the company's incumbent corrugate box supplier with the following goals:

1. Negotiate the price more in line with what supplier costs have actually increased (23.45%)
2. Develop a more accurate pricing model based on the findings of this cost modeling exercise
3. Amend the contract to utilize the cost model to ensure future price adjustments reflect actual cost fluctuations
4. Attempt to recoup some of the costs incurred as a result of the faulty existing pricing model

In the event the incumbent supplier does not negotiate in good faith to bring costs into greater alignment, the category manager recommends bidding the business with a clear focus on gathering a competitive price while ensuring the pricing model for the future aligns with supplier cost outlays. The leadership team endorses the strategic approach and expresses their interest in learning of the final outcome.

The case study on corrugated boxes is based on a real application of the procured materials cost model for a major specialty retailer. Though the names were changed, this retailer was able to garner substantial savings through the use of the cost model output in negotiations. Ultimately, the incumbent supplier could present no facts to refute the findings of the cost model and actually admitted that margins had increased under the existing pricing model. Between the facts of the model and the threat of a bid, the incumbent supplier did lower their prices to be in alignment with what the model justified. Additionally, the incumbent supplier did agree to adopt a pricing model very similar to the cost model constructed to determine the go-forward price. Lastly, some credit dollars were given to DEF Body in the form of a sign-on bonus to assist in compensating for the previous flawed price structure.

Conclusion

This chapter has discussed the in-depth development and use of procured material cost models. These models are powerful tools and understanding how to create and utilize them will assist any organization with ensuring cost competitiveness in material purchases. Procured material cost models can be further enhanced by integrating specific information regarding the material the organization is buying into the fold to increase the validity of the model for its intended use. For example, the category manager could have increased the specificity of his company's product model had he gathered additional information about his company's own boxes and how they related to the raw material consumption. Were the category manager to discover the number of boxes that could be created per ton of linerboard and medium, he could have utilized those figures to specifically model the cost for that specific box. That information is not something he can attain without discussions with the supplier, which can be collected either via conversations, site visits, or RFIs and RFPs. The case study in chapter 6 will introduce how the bidding process may be used to enhance the accuracy and value of cost models in the competitive process for procured services. Those same principles can be applied in procured materials as well.

CHAPTER 6

External Cost Models for Procured Services

Errors using inadequate data are much less than those using no data at all.

—Charles Babbage

As discussed in chapter 5, external cost models are developed by a procurement and supply chain organization to gain insight into supplier costs for procured materials and services. Chapter 5 focused on the development and use of procured material cost models to ensure costs are competitive and discussions are based on factual data. This chapter will focus on the other prevalent external cost model type, procured service cost models.

Though procured material and procured service cost models utilize many of the same principles to create and apply them with suppliers, there are some differences we will discuss in this chapter. Additionally, through the example explored in this chapter, we will integrate the industry cost model data with the company-specific operations data to increase the model's accuracy. Lastly, we will explore how external cost models can be integrated into the strategic sourcing process to attain maximum value by using the procured service example in this chapter.

Procured Service Cost Models

Procured service cost models are utilized to understand the cost structures of any third-party service providers. These can range from services as simple as janitorial to the complexity of specialized engineering. The construction of these cost models is approached in the same basic manner as for procured material cost models and for the same purposes: to ensure that pricing is based on actual cost outlays with a fair profit margin.

To illustrate the value of constructing procured service cost models, we will use a real example of how one was utilized in a strategic sourcing initiative on bulk haul trucking. This example will show the real power of utilizing cost models early in the process and throughout to garner the greatest value. The example used throughout this chapter is based on one of the author's experiences and introduces the procured service to be modeled.

Example 6.1. LMN Energy Trucking Costs

One of the first assignments for the new strategic sourcing manager for LMN Energy is to assist the supply chain organization deal with the escalating bulk trucking costs of petroleum coke from one of the refineries. His role on the project team will be to facilitate the entire strategic sourcing process in this category to derive the best value for the enterprise.

In conducting his initial analysis of contract structure, the strategic sourcing manager discovers that the existing contract pricing is based on a fixed dollar amount per ton with fuel built in at $1.25. If diesel fuel prices rise above $1.25, a separate fuel surcharge mechanism is utilized to compensate the carrier for those fuel fluctuations. Analyzing the spend, the strategic sourcing manager finds that presently, over $11 million is spent trucking 420,000 tons of petroleum coke from the refinery to the port terminal. Burdened with rate and fuel costs, the refinery is paying $25.20/ton to ship the petroleum coke 61 miles one way. With his first thought for improvement being a cheaper mode of transportation, he quickly discovers that the rail capacity at the refinery is limited, so trucking is the only available option until a railroad expansion can be funded and built.

The strategic sourcing manager knows a key part of the strategic sourcing process is a thorough understanding of the costs of the product or service being sourced, so he begins constructing an industry-procured service cost model using the process in Figure 6.1.

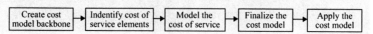

Figure 6.1. Procured service cost model process.

Create the Cost Model Backbone

The first step in developing a procured service cost model is no different than with the procured material cost model: Identify a backbone resource in which to build the base model. The Economic Census and Risk Management Association's *RMA's Annual Statement Studies* could be utilized to formulate a rough baseline; however, there is another resource with greater detail available through the Federal Motor Carrier Safety Administration (FMCSA). Exercising due diligence in the selection of the best source can shorten the modeling time and increase its accuracy.

On an annualized basis, the FMCSA requires a Form M survey to be completed by thousands of motor carriers on items that include profit and loss statement information, balance sheet information, and a number of operating statistics. This information is not publicly available online through the FMCSA, but older versions of the data collected from 1999 to 2003 are available through the Bureau of Transportation Statistics. In order to obtain the most current data on motor carriers, a Freedom of Information Act (FOIA) request must be made in writing to the FMCSA.[1] Not all carriers are required to complete Form M, so when making a request it is generally best to specify the type of freight, mode of freight, and specialty freight type (if applicable). For purposes of this example, a request should be made for a carrier who provided truckload (mode), bulk haul (freight type) of coal/coke product (specialty freight type) for the previous reporting year. The requests take approximately 1 month to be filled and returned, so making the request early is important to ensure project timelines are not jeopardized. Figure 6.2 illustrates the mean values for the income statement data returned and will be utilized for the backbone of the cost model.

With current income statement information from the FMCSA, the need to extrapolate costs forward is eliminated as opposed to what was necessary on the procured material cost model in chapter 5. This also provides unquestionable accuracy as to the data used to build the industry cost model.

	Mean values from Form M	Percent of revenue
TOTAL OPERATING REVENUE	$ 32,006,664	100.00%
Driver & Helper Wages (W-2 Emp)-Excl 1099 O-O Drvr Comp	$ 5,490,746	17.16%
officer, Supervisor, Administrative, & Clerical Wages & Salaries	$ 1,595,802	4.99%
Other Wages & Salaries	$ 616,517	1.93%
Fringe Bene;Incl Fed/State/Loc Payrl Tax,Wkrs Comp,Grp Insur,Oth	$ 1,858,207	5.81%
Eqpmt Rentals With Drivers—AP For Use Rev Vehs & Drivers (O-O)	$ 4,725,794	14.77%
Purchsd Transpn—Cost (Haul Carr Controls Veh & Drvr)	$ 4,892,764	15.29%
TOTAL LABOR (INCLUDES OWNER / OPERATORS)	$ 19,179,830	59.92%
Fuel, Oil & Lubric;Incl Gas,Diesel,Oil,Grease,Lubes,Coolants	$ 2,761,290	8.63%
Outside Maintenance-Maint Perf By Outside Vendors	$ 840,414	2.63%
Vehicle Parts—Parts Used To Repair Vehs, Excl Tires and Tubes	$ 527,926	1.65%
Tires & Tubes—Cost of Tires & Tubes For Vehs	$ 348,617	1.09%
Other Op Supplies & Expenses—Op of Vehs, Terminals, Shops	$ 925,122	2.89%
TOTAL CONSUMABLES / MAINTENANCE	$ 5,403,369	16.88%
Cargo Loss & Damg Prems & Claims Pd—Net Cost of Commrc Insur	$ 71,261	0.22%
Liabil & Prop Damg Prems & Claims Pd—Cost of Commrc Insur	$ 936,171	2.92%
Other Insur Exp—Fire,Theft,Floods; Incl Insur For Bldgs,Machi	$ 203,884	0.64%
TOTAL INSURANCE EXPENSES	$ 1,211,316	3.78%
Fuel Taxes—Fed & State On Gas, Diesel, and Oil	$ 289,209	0.90%
Op Tax & Lic (Exc Fuel Tx) -Lic&Reg Fees, Tolls, Veh Use Taxes	$ 354,037	1.11%
Deprec & Amortizn Chgs-For Rev Equip, Bldg. & Improv, etc.	$ 1,245,430	3.89%
Eqpmt Rentals Without Drivers—AP For Use of Rev Vehs Only	$ 1,086,772	3.40%
Communica & Utilities—Cost Plus Taxes (Telephone, Fax, Etc)	$ 366,165	1.14%
Oth Op Exp-Bldg. Rents,off Equp Rents; Excl Interest & Sales Tax	$ 1,706,367	5.33%
OTHER OPERATING EXPENSES	$ 5,047,980	15.77%
NET OPERATING INCOME / LOSS	$ 1,164,168	3.64%

Figure 6.2. Income statement.

Identify the Cost of Service Elements

The accurate income statement data now must be utilized to formulate a functioning procured service cost model. In order to do this, a determination of what items on the income statement compose cost of service (COS) needs to be completed. COS will be all the components directly modeled for the procured service of interest to LMN Energy. Figure 6.3 displays those elements that will be directly modeled for the business.

The data shows that 65.95% of all the expenses affiliated with conducting this type of service business will be directly modeled. Specifically, the procured service cost model will actively model driver labor, equipment depreciation and amortization, any purchased transportation, and fuel. The remaining components will be applied based on the percentage of the industry's revenue they constitute. That will be illustrated later in the chapter.

	Mean values from Form M	Percent of revenue
Driver & Helper Wages (W-2 Emp)-Excl 1099 O-O Drvr Comp	$ 5,490,746	17.16%
Other Wages & Salaries	$ 616,517	1.93%
Eqpmt Rentals With Drivers—AP For Use Rev Vehs & Drivers (O-O)	$ 4,725,794	14.77%
Purchsd Transpn—Cost (Haulg Carr Controls Veh & Drvr)	$ 4,892,764	15.29%
Fuel, Oil & Lubric;Incl Gas,Diesel,Oil,Grease,Lubes,Coolants	$ 2,761,290	8.63%
Fuel Taxes—Fed & State On Gas, Diesel, and Oil	$ 289,209	0.90%
Deprec & Amortizn Chgs-For Rev Equip, Bldg. & Improv, etc.	$ 1,245,430	3.89%
Eqpmt Rentals Without Drivers—AP For Use of Rev Vehs Only	$ 1,086,772	3.40%
COST COMPONENTS DIRECTLY MODELED (COS)	**$ 21,108,522**	**65.95%**

Figure 6.3. Cost components directly modeled.

Model the Cost of Service

To collect the initial cost components for modeling, a number of resources are used. For driver labor costs, the Bureau of Labor Statistics (BLS) Occupational Employment and Wage Estimates resource should be utilized for the latest reporting year by the most appropriate NAICS code. NAICS code 484100 was utilized to obtain truck driver wages. Because of the emphasis on safety at the refining location and the close scrutiny of drivers for servicing this business, the 75th percentile wage rate of $22.63 per hour rather than the median wage rate was taken for use in the model. In certain instances it may be beneficial to unbundle wage rates to account more specifically for various benefits and applicable taxes.

To derive the fuel cost in the model, a few components must be known: the cost of diesel fuel, the average fuel economy of a loaded truck, and the average fuel economy of an empty truck. To obtain information on the price of diesel fuel, the most commonly referenced source is the U.S. Energy Information Administration's Weekly Retail On-Highway Diesel Prices. As its name implies, it provides weekly updates on diesel prices by region. To discover the average fuel economy for a tractor truck, visiting a few manufacturer websites provides some valid data points to reference. Two conservative points identified were 5 miles per gallon loaded and 6 miles per gallon empty.

Deriving tractor truck and trailer depreciation and amortization costs begins with gaining an understanding of the purchase price for each. There are wide-ranging costs for tractor trucks and trailers depending on the services being rendered. Identification of these factors is important because the purchase price can vary greatly depending on the application. In this instance, the incumbent business provider utilizes contracted owner-operators, meaning drivers who own their own tractor trucks. The vast majority of owner-operators own tractor trucks that have sleep compartments and thus are more expensive. For the purposes of the model, some online searches of dealers provided a typical purchase price of $108,000 for the tractor truck. Applying a similar approach to understand the purchase price of a dump trailer utilized for this business yielded a $50,000 typical price tag. For the purposes of the amortization schedule, a 7% interest rate over 5 years was assumed.

The price tag of labor per hour and of a trailer and a tractor are key pieces of information needed to create a model, but time is the other piece. Time spent on the haul is necessary to calculate the cost of each of those components per load hauled. This is where activity-based costing (ABC) is employed to a larger degree than in many other external cost models. Modeling a service conducted at least partially at your facility, as in this instance, provides the opportunity to assign time and assumed costs to the activities being conducted, similar to some of the internal cost models. However, instead of utilizing this information to see what you should charge a customer to make a fair profit, you are utilizing the information to determine if you are paying a fair price. Example 6.2 follows the LMN Energy strategic sourcing manager and how he collects the remaining information needed and utilizes the information collected to begin the construction of the model.

Example 6.2. Collecting Cost Model Data

The strategic sourcing manager has collected all the publicly available information he needs to better understand the area he is sourcing. His next task is to collect the necessary inputs from his stakeholders in the business to refine the inputs in the cost model. With the knowledge of wages paid to drivers and equipment purchase costs, he now needs to know more about the operation itself to apply those costs. Discussions with stakeholders in the supply chain organization led to the operating hours of the business to be 5 days a week for 11 hours. Additionally, the stakeholders shared that their typical carriers depreciate tractor trucks and trailers 5 and 7 years respectively using the straight-line method. This information will provide some of the basis for extrapolating labor, depreciation, and amortization rates per haul.

In order to truly model the operation accurately, the next step is to visit the refinery location, witness the operation in motion, and talk with those available about it. Prior to this visit, the strategic sourcing manager formulated a list of questions he needed answered in order to effectively model this space and to create a thorough statement of work (SOW) for inclusion in the request for proposal (RFP) to be released later.

Questions:
1. What is the average number of loads per day of the tractor trailers?
2. What is the average number of tons/load shipped?
3. What is the average load time per load (including entering and exiting refinery)?
4. What is the average transit time per load to the port terminal?
5. What is the average unload time per load at the port terminal?
6. What is the average transit time per load back to the refinery?

The strategic sourcing manager arrived early at the refinery location to see the operation from the beginning of the day. While he and the team made their way to the loading area, they noticed that there was a line of 25 or 30 tractor trailers waiting to load. This raised immediate red flags as it pertains to the costs incurred for an inefficient process. By interviewing the loading crew and several drivers, as well as reviewing their own observations at the loading and unloading locations, the strategic sourcing manager and the team were able to collect the following information for use in the cost model and SOW.

Average number of daily loads	=	3	Loads
Average tons / load	=	23	Tons
Average load time	=	60	Minutes
Average transit time to port	=	90	Minutes
Average unload time	=	20	Minutes
Average return transit time	=	90	Minutes

All the information needed to create an initial cost model is now in the strategic sourcing manager's possession to assist in determining if the price currently being paid aligns with supplier cost outlays as well as provides a reasonable profit.

Creating a dashboard user interface for the inputs that quickly illustrates any assumption change on output results will be the method followed as the model is built. In building the model, we will calculate what the dollar per load should be compared with our current price; however, as we are performing the calculations, we will convert our per minute and hour calculations to cost per minute and the diesel price to cost per mile.

In the case study, we learned the typical depreciation method and time frame utilized for both tractor trucks and trailers. In order to calculate the depreciation expense per load for both the tractor truck and trailer, the following formula should be utilized:

	Purchase price	÷	Depreciation years	÷	Working days	÷	Working hours	÷	Minute conversion	=	Depreciation expense/minute
Truck	$108,000	÷	5	÷	250	÷	11	÷	60	=	$0.13
Trailer	$50,000	÷	7	÷	250	÷	11	÷	60	=	$0.04

The calculation of amortization expenses begins with the creation of an amortization schedule. This can be easily created within Microsoft Excel by utilizing three key functions: PMT, IPMT, and PPMT. PMT calculates the full payment by month consisting of both interest and principle for the loan; IPMT calculates only the interest payment by month, which is of greatest interest here; and PPMT calculates the principal payment by month. Figure 6.4 illustrates the output of utilizing these formulas for a small subset of all the payments with the formula for each calculation.

Once the total interest expenditures over the life of the loans are known for both the tractor truck and trailer, they can both be converted to expenses per minute for use in the cost model. This is done very similarly to the calculation for depreciation expenses, as the following shows:

Total interest	÷	Amortization years	÷	Working days	÷	Working hours	÷	Minute conversion	=	Amortization expense/minute
$20,311.77	÷	5	÷	250	÷	11	÷	60	=	$0.025
$9,403.60	÷	5	÷	250	÷	11	÷	60	=	$0.011

Tractor Trailer Loan Data

Principal	$108,000	**Total Interest**
Loan Term	5	**$20,311.77**
Interest Rate	7.00%	
Annual Pmts	12	
Payment	$2,138.53	

Month	Payment	Interest	Principal	Balance
0				$108,000.00
1	$2,138.53	$630.00	$1,508.53	$106,491.47
2	$2,138.53	$621.20	$1,517.33	$104,974.14
3	$2,138.53	$612.35	$1,526.18	$103,447.96
4	$2,138.53	$603.45	$1,535.08	$101,912.88
5	$2,138.53	$594.49	$1,544.04	$100,368.84
6	$2,138.53	$585.48	$1,553.04	$98,815.80
7	$2,138.53	$576.43	$1,562.10	$97,253.69
8	$2,138.53	$567.31	$1,571.22	$95,682.48
9	$2,138.53	$558.15	$1,580.38	$94,102.09
10	$2,138.53	$548.93	$1,589.60	$92,512.49
11	$2,138.53	$539.66	$1,598.87	$90,913.62
12	$2,138.53	$530.33	$1,608.20	$89,305.42

FORMULAS

PMT	=PMT(Interest_Rate / Annual_Pmts, Loan_Term * Annual_Pmts, -Principal)
IPMT	=IPMT(Interest_Rate / Annual_Pmts, Month, Loan_Term * Annual Pmts, - Principal)
PPMT	=PPMT(Interest_Rate / Annual_Pmts, Month, Loan_Term * Annual Pmts, - Principal)

Figure 6.4. Amortization schedule.

Converting driver wages from a per-hour calculation to a per-minute calculation is also needed. Once the wages are converted, the final piece of the calculation is to convert diesel prices from dollars per gallon to dollars per mile. With knowledge of the typical tractor truck gas mileage both loaded and empty, calculating the dollar per mile is completed as follows:

	Gallon price of diesel	÷	Miles per gallon	=	Dollar/Mile
Loaded	$3.07	÷	5	=	$0.61
Empty	$3.07	÷	6	=	$0.51

Now that all the logic has been built to perform the calculations in the cost model, the next part would be to design the best organizational format for the model. The collection of time for each operational component is broken down into loading, transit to port, unloading, and the return trip to the refinery. That logical break down allows for a more granular view into where costs may be hidden and provides a nice framework for the model output itself. Once those individual costs are calculated, the total of direct costs or COS should be known for inclusion in the final model. Figure 6.5 illustrates how the cost model may be represented.

Finalize the Cost Model

Figure 6.5 provides the COS component of the cost model, but one must apply the industry average percentages collected and calculated from the FMCSA Form M data for the model to be complete. Earlier in this section, the full income statement was shown as provided from the Form Ms. Additionally, the specific items to be modeled as COS were illustrated with their associated percentage. Now we need to see the percentage value of the COS as well as the other operating expenses and profit. Figure 6.6 provides a full break down and percentage based on the earlier displayed income statement.

The percentages for each cost component represented in Figure 6.6 are calculated as a percentage of revenue. Since the problem we are attempting to solve is the justifiable revenue for the business being conducted, this is the unknown variable for which we must use basic mathematics to solve. The variables we do know to assist in solving this problem are the percentage that COS constituted in the income statement (65.95%) and the cost calculated in the model for our business ($221.39). Deriving the value of the revenue for this business then can be calculated with the following formula:

$$\frac{\text{Cost of sales}}{\text{Cost of sales percentage}} = \text{Revenue}$$

$$\frac{\$221.39}{65.95\%} = \$335.69$$

The last two steps to completing the procured service cost model is to calculate the values for the nonmodeled components by calculating their percentage times the revenue and then to incorporate that into the final dashboard. Figure 6.7 shows the finalized procured services cost model dashboard.

DIRECT COSTS (COS)

Purchase price
Tractor Truck	1	$108,000 Ttl
Dump Trailer	1	$50,000 Ttl

Depreciation (5 Days / Week, 11 Hrs / Day)
Tractor Truck	5 Years - Straight Line
Dump Trailer	7 Years - Straight Line

Amortization (5 Days / Week, 11 Hrs / Day)
Tractor Truck	7.00%	5 Interest & Years
Dump Trailer	7.00%	5 Interest & Years

Labor Costs
Retained Driver Wage	$ 22.63 Per Hour

Fuel Costs
Diesel	$3.07 Per Gallon
Loaded	5.0 Miles/Gallon
Empty	6.0 Miles/Gallon

Route Time & Distance
Annual Working Days	250 Days
Daily Working Hours	11 Hours
Average Load Time	60 Minutes
Average Transit Time to Port	90 Minutes
Average Unload Time	20 Minutes
Average Return Transit Time	90 Minutes
Loaded Trip Distance	61 Miles
Empty Trip Distance	61 Miles
Average Tons / Load	23 Tons

Calculations

		Load	Port Trip	Unload	Return Trip
Depr Exp / Min	$0.131	$ 7.85	$ 11.78	$ 2.62	$ 11.78
Depr Exp / Min	$0.043	$ 2.60	$ 3.90	$ 0.87	$ 3.90
Int Exp / Min	$0.025	$ 1.48	$ 2.22	$ 0.49	$ 2.22
Int Exp / Min	$0.011	$ 0.68	$ 1.03	$ 0.23	$ 1.03
Wage Exp / Min	$0.377	$ 22.63	$ 33.95	$ 7.54	$ 33.95
Loaded Fuel Cost / Mile	$0.61		$ 37.45		
Empty Fuel Cost / Mile	$0.51				$ 31.21
		$ 35.24	$ 90.32	$ 11.75	$ 84.08

	Rate & Fuel	Rate Only
COS	$ 221.39	$ 152.72

INPUTS
CALCULATIONS
OUTPUT

Figure 6.5. COS components of cost model in Excel.

	Mean Values from Form M	Percent of Revenue
Driver & Helper Wages (W-2 Emp)-Excl 1099 O-O Drvr Comp	$ 5,490,746	17.16%
Other Wages & Salaries	$ 616,517	1.93%
Eqpmt Rentals With Drivers - AP For Use Rev Vehs & Drivers (O-O)	$ 4,725,794	14.77%
Purchsd Transpn - Cost (Haulg Carr Controls Veh & Drvr)	$ 4,892,764	15.29%
Fuel, Oil & Lubric;Incl Gas,Diesel,Oil,Grease,Lubes,Coolants	$ 2,761,290	8.63%
Fuel Taxes - Fed & State On Gas, Diesel, And Oil	$ 289,209	0.90%
Deprec & Amortizn Chgs-For Rev Equip, Bldg & Improv, etc	$ 1,245,430	3.89%
Eqpmt Rentals Without Drivers - AP For Use Of Rev Vehs Only	$ 1,086,772	3.40%
COST COMPONENTS DIRECTLY MODELED (COS)	**$ 21,108,522**	**65.95%**

	Mean Values from Form M	Percent of Revenue
Outside Maintenance-Maint Perf By Outside Vendors	$ 840,414	2.63%
Vehicle Parts - Parts Used To Repair Vehs, Excl Tires And Tubes	$ 527,926	1.65%
Tires & Tubes - Cost Of Tires & Tubes For Vehs	$ 348,617	1.09%
Other Op Supplies & Expenses - Op Of Vehs, Terminals, Shops	$ 925,122	2.89%
Total Consumables / Maintenance	*$ 2,642,079*	*8.25%*
Cargo Loss & Damg Prems & Claims Pd - Net Cost Of Commrc Insur	$ 71,261	0.22%
Liabil & Prop Damg Prems & Claims Pd - Cost Of Commrc Insur	$ 936,171	2.92%
Other Insur Exp - Fire,Theft,Floods; Incl Insur For Bldgs,Machi	$ 203,884	0.64%
Total Insurance	*$ 1,211,316*	*3.78%*
Op Tax & Lic (Exc Fuel Tx) -Lic&Reg Fees, Tolls, Veh Use Taxes	$ 354,037	1.11%
Communica & Utilities - Cost Plus Taxes (Telephone, Fax, Etc)	$ 366,165	1.14%
Oth Op Exp-Bldg Rents,Off Equp Rents; Excl Interest & Sales Tax	$ 1,706,367	5.33%
Officer, Supervisor, Administrative, & Clerical Wages & Salaries	$ 1,595,802	4.99%
Fringe Bene;Incl Fed/State/Loc Payrl Tax,Wkrs Comp,Grp Insur,Oth	$ 1,858,207	5.81%
Total Other Operating Expenses	*$ 5,880,578*	*18.37%*
Net Profit	*$ 1,164,168*	*3.64%*
COST COMPONENTS NOT DIRECTLY MODELED	**$ 10,898,142**	**34.05%**

Figure 6.6. Cost components modeled and not modeled.

Depending on the business being modeled, the cost model could be further refined to account for such things as utilization percentages for drivers and equipment. If the equipment is not fully dedicated to an operation and/or there is significant unproductive time for both drivers and equipment, then those costs should be factored into the model. Another area that may need to be considered is the age of the fleet that services the business; because the business modeled in Figure 6.5 required virtually all new equipment for all the carriers, the amortization/depreciation schedule for new equipment was deemed appropriate. In instances where older equipment or refurbished equipment might be used, that should be used as a factor of consideration in the model. Additionally, if the equipment's useful life exceeds the depreciation schedule, the useful life number should be strongly considered for use in the model calculations. For example, if the dump trailer has an average useful life of 10 years, that

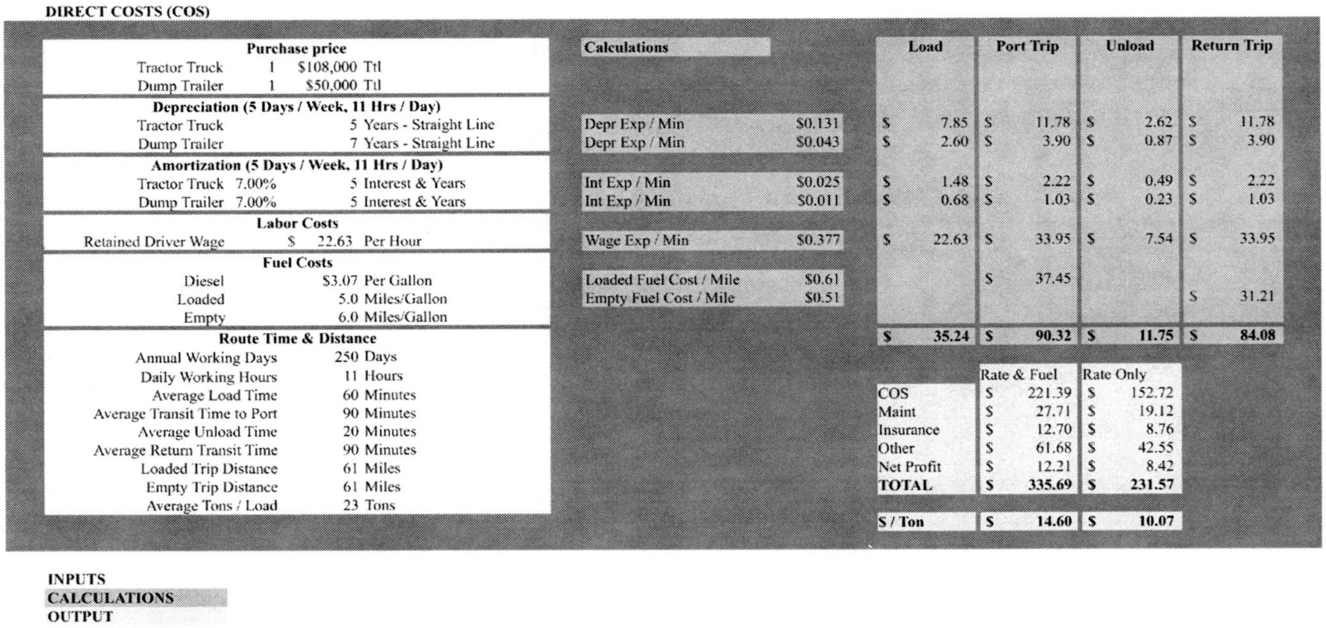

Figure 6.7. Finalized procured services cost model dashboard in Excel.

figure more accurately portrays the revenue life before refurbishment or replacement is needed. Lastly, the salvage value of the equipment could be accounted for in the model to lower the overall equipment expenses to be more in line with carrier cost outlays.

Apply the Cost Model

The output of the model shows a substantial difference between the present rates LMN Energy is paying and the modeled costs for hauling petroleum coke by truck. The fully burdened rate inclusive of fuel surcharges is modeled at $14.60/ton. Earlier the cost per ton reported during the spend analysis was $25.20/ton, so from an opportunity assessment standpoint, this appears to be an area with significant potential. Example 6.3 shows how the strategic sourcing manager utilizes this information within the strategic sourcing process.

Example 6.3. The Value Proposition/Savings Results

With the completion of the cost model, the strategic sourcing manager is pleased to see there is a substantial opportunity to add value by employing the strategic sourcing process. Because there is such a large difference between the modeled cost and the current rate, he takes a deeper dive into the components of the current $25.20/ton fully burdened rate. What he discovers is that one area responsible for the large difference is the current fuel surcharge schedule in place. Currently, $1.25 of fuel costs is encompassed in the rate for shipping, but when diesel exceeds that amount, fuel surcharges are charged back to LMN Energy. This fuel surcharge is based on a percentage of the present rate and the price of diesel at the present published rate from the U.S. Energy Information Administration's Weekly Retail

On-Highway Diesel Prices. Below is an example of how the fuel surcharge is calculated.

Diesel Fuel Cost

Over	Less than	% of rate charge
2.650	2.699	26.62
2.700	2.749	27.73
2.750	2.799	28.84
2.800	2.849	29.95
2.850	2.899	31.06
2.900	2.949	32.17
2.950	2.999	33.28
3.000	3.049	34.39
3.050	3.099	35.40
3.100	3.149	36.52
3.150	3.199	37.63

Based on the present prices of diesel fuel, fuel surcharges equating to 34.39% of the rate are being charged to LMN Energy. With the current base rate less fuel surcharges being $18.61/ton, $6.59 is being charged in fuel surcharges above and beyond the $1.25/ton already present in the base rate. This base rate and fuel surcharges combined fully account for the $25.20 fully burdened rate. Because the strategic sourcing manager has built a dynamic model, he can calculate the difference the current fuel surcharge structure has versus what his model says it should cost. What he finds is that the fuel surcharge presently being charged is approximately 3 times greater than the model can justify, which works out to a difference of nearly $100 per load (with the average haul being 25 tons). Further, he finds that the higher the diesel price, the larger the difference between the current fuel surcharge and modeled fuel surcharge. The following chart shows the impact of diesel price fluctuations on out-of-pocket costs:

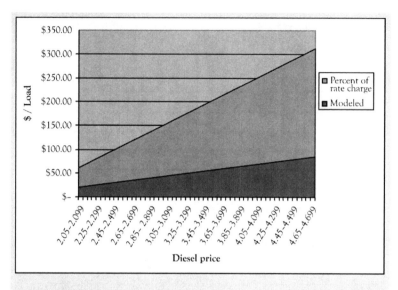

In addition to the fuel discrepancy, the strategic sourcing manager and the team wanted to have a greater understanding of why the fleet of trucks was able to have first-load wait times of up to 4 hours without additional demurrage charges. Because those wait times were factored into the rate, the refinery was not concerned with the inefficient process. However, the strategic sourcing manager and the team knew that "time is money," and the refinery was paying for that inefficiency, even if they didn't recognize it as a separate charge item.

Prior to finalizing the scope and issuing the RFP to potential truck carriers, the team had all bid participants come to the refinery facility to review the operation. The team ensured all participants that LMN Energy was looking to enter into a strategic relationship with a carrier that was able to provide the service safely and cost effectively and that removing inefficiencies from the existing operation was encouraged.

The RFP included questions pertaining to all the cost elements modeled so that pricing had to be backed up with sound cost information. Additionally, a new fuel surcharge was stipulated, compensating on a per-mile basis as the standard post-bid to ensure that fuel surcharges incurred were more indicative of carrier cost outlays. The procured service cost model arrived at a cost within 8% of the finalized agreement with the selected supplier. Were the team to have been able to contract for a longer period, the negotiated rate would have been within 1% of the modeled cost. The following discussion tracks the progress of the negotiations based on the cost model:

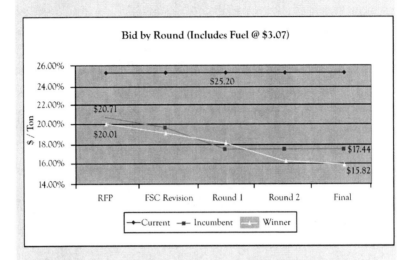

Initial bids received showed a dramatic decrease in the dollar per ton rate compared to the historical baseline pricing. The model was utilized to determine that an alternative fuel surcharge schedule should be implemented that would provide further cost reduction, which can be seen in the chart. Lastly, the information was used for the purposes of clarifying assumptions made by the carriers and to negotiate competitive pricing based largely on their own inputs. As the graph shows, dramatic decreases in price per ton were obtained from the RFP to the final negotiated figure. The result of the strategic sourcing initiative, with the use of the cost model, was a 37% decrease in the fully burdened rate to move petroleum coke.

At the conclusion of the negotiations, the strategic sourcing manager and the team were pleased to award the business to a carrier that would bring safe and efficient operations while saving LMN Energy over $12 million over a 3-year term.

Greater Volume Equals Greater Leverage

The ability to negotiate better pricing using cost models is enhanced when the purchasing organization does a substantial volume of business with the supplier organization. In the example discussed in this chapter, the buying organization should expect that the transportation supplier can achieve a higher utilization of equipment and drivers as the volume of their business increases. This could positively impact what the supplier considers to be an acceptable margin versus other, lower volume customers. Supply chain professionals can utilize this knowledge and information to their advantage in a negotiating environment, particularly if the utilization of the specific equipment to support the business bid is higher than typical utilization statistics (which can be captured in an RFI or RFP). If utilization rates are higher, the astute supply chain professional can incorporate that fact into the model to provide a clearer indication of supplier/carrier costs.

However, when negotiating with the use of external cost models, the areas often determined to have the biggest impact on total cost are the indirect cost components (SG&A and profit being the most significant). If these components are high and out of line with industry standards, costs to buying organizations can be drastically higher. Since executive wages and bonuses are buried within the SG&A component of service pricing, it is essential that supply chain professionals analyze both the SG&A and profit lines together. The case example in this chapter on trucking is a perfect illustration. It is uncommon for privately held carriers (or suppliers for that matter) to report large profits that are carried over into retained earnings year after year. Rather, those excess profits are actually paid out or cashed out by the owners of the company and its executives. Only a small percentage of those excess profits may reside in the net profit line, so "buyer beware" if you decide to only analyze the profit line.

Additionally, when a buying organization represents a considerable percentage or substantive volume of business compared to supplier/carrier revenues, the buying organization should expect to fund a lower percentage of the supplier's overall SG&A costs. Why is that? Because when suppliers have to sell on the spot market (i.e., nonstrategic/preferred relationships), there is a higher burden associated with that activity. Marketing costs are the most prevalently averted category, but other SG&A costs may be reduced as well with larger revenue accounts.

Conclusion

The procured service cost model provided tremendous leverage to the LMN Energy strategic sourcing team. Not only did the model validate the opportunity, but it also seized the opportunity and ensured that bid responses made sense with the industry data collected. In a negotiating environment, the value of fact-based tools cannot be minimized. When discussions around price are based on the costs you have analyzed and the information bidders have provided in an RFP, "black box" or blinded negotiating tactics that highly favor the carrier/supplier are eliminated. This also helps to avoid situations where bidders may be trying to "buy the business" by proposing unsustainable prices that cannot be justified by the costs prevalent in that industry. Avoiding situations where at a minimum costs will escalate and at worst the supplier either fails entirely or requires the team to re-source prior to the planned time frame can be minimized using cost models.

This chapter has discussed in depth the development and use of procured service cost models. Building these models and enhancing the data inputs with actual service information collected empirically and through a bid process can allow the buying organization to wield substantial power. Tailoring the models as much as possible to your operation helps to ensure that the external product or activity being modeled is reflective of your business, not just the industry as a whole. However, utilizing cost models should be just one part of an overall supply chain or strategic sourcing strategy for a category that will glean the largest value for buying organizations. External cost models such as these are some of the strongest tools, but other tools in the strategic sourcing toolkit should also be used to enhance the final product of the initiative even further.

CHAPTER 7

Total Cost of Ownership Models

For many companies, total cost of ownership (TCO) is out of control.

—Dr. Wayne Applebaum

End the practice of awarding business on the basis of price tag alone.

—W. Edwards Deming

In previous chapters models of varying type, both internal and external, have been explained in detail to assist organizational decision making. Most of the emphasis when completing those models was on the direct costs associated with the operation or procured product/service. Total cost of ownership (TCO) models focus on all the costs associated with a particular operation or acquisition over its entire life span, cradle to grave. Generally, these models are used most in conjunction with the other models discussed in situations where either major capital expenditures or dramatic operational changes are being considered.

It is very important to include all relevant costs when developing a TCO model, which is sometimes referred to as a value creation model. Exclusion of even one component can sometimes lead to suboptimal decisions. Example 7.1, taken from one of the author's experiences, illustrates the impact of failing to include a critical cost element.

Example 7.1. TCO Analysis Case Study

The organization had been purchasing a particular raw material from a single supplier, Supplier A, for a number of years. The component was assembled into the final product using automated equipment. Never had one of Supplier A's lots of the material been rejected due to nonconformance to specifications. An unsolicited offer was received from Supplier B for the same material. This price for the material from Supplier B was significantly lower than the price from Supplier A. Quality engineering tested Supplier B's material and determined that it conformed to all specifications. The purchasing manager then constructed a TCO model and determined that Supplier B's offer was worth considering. Supplier A was approached and was unable to offer any price concessions. The decision was made and the organization switched to Supplier B for this material.

The initial shipments from Supplier B all conformed to specifications. The month after the switch to Supplier B, process engineering reported excessive downtime with the equipment that assembled this material into the final product. Investigation indicated the cause for the downtime was related to the material from Supplier B. Further investigation revealed that, while all of Supplier B's material conformed to specification, the distribution for a critical dimension had a significantly higher variance than that from Supplier A. It was determined that this excess variation created jamming problems with the automated equipment.

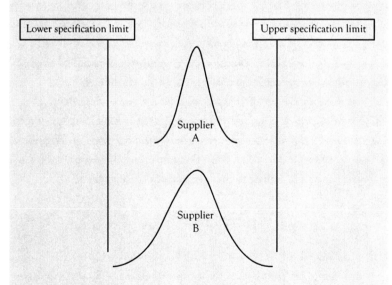

Attempts to adjust the equipment to accommodate Supplier B's material were unsuccessful. Since the cost of the downtime on the equipment greatly exceeded the savings from switching suppliers, the purchasing manager ceased purchasing from Supplier B and returned to Supplier A.

Several actions could have avoided this problem. A more thorough examination by quality engineering beyond simple conformance to specifications would have revealed the increased dimensional variation in Supplier B's material. A pilot test of the new material on the automated equipment by process engineering would have revealed the problems associated with the increased dimensional variation. With this information, the purchasing manager could have included the additional costs of downtime on the automated equipment in his TCO model and made the correct decision to remain with Supplier A.

Understanding the total cost of any operation or product decision should begin with thoughtful framework sessions. The basics of framework sessions were discussed in Example 2.1 in chapter 2, where it focused on whether outsourcing unfolding, hanging, and steaming activities was more advantageous than insourcing incorporated several elements of TCO modeling. Had XYZ Apparel, the company that was the focus of the example, made the decision based solely on labor costs, the probability of achieving the best outcome would have decreased. Instead the model analyzed the impact of packaging, transportation, and custom costs while also quantifying an opportunity cost for each decision. Decision quality is focused on ensuring that all available information is considered and vetted in the decision-making process. While the model in Example 2.1 is designed to determine the total one-time cost of a product or service, TCO models are constructed to identify and quantify each component of cost over the lifetime of the project, product, or service and thus enhance decision quality.

At the highest level, a TCO model should contain all the costs associated with acquiring, installing, operating, maintaining, and disposing of a product or service while considering all applicable opportunity costs. The best example to illustrate the importance of organizations focusing on TCO, as opposed to single elements such as purchase price, is an iceberg. Ninety percent of an iceberg's size and mass lies beneath the surface of the water; the 10% of the TCO that can be seen is generally related to making decisions based solely on price. That is to say that 90% of the potential cost or value is overlooked by making a decision based solely on price.

While the actual percentages and TCO categories will vary depending on the nature of the product or service, what the value pyramid iceberg in Figure 7.1 truly illustrates is that a failure to focus on the areas outside of acquisition cost (or price) may result in a recommendation not in the best interests of the organization. Often organizations expend a great deal of time and effort to ensure that the purchase price is competitive and fair, but the same time and effort need to be in place to ensure the solution that is priced competitively is also the most advantageous for the organization over the entire useful life of the product or service. Falling in love with a solution based on the sticker price may result in a decision that has a greater probability of having an adverse effect on the expected result.

Like icebergs, the vast majority of the value proposition associated with projects under consideration falls below the surface. Depending on the product, service, or project being considered, the components themselves or the size of those components can vary greatly. For example, when buying a car the price tag is of definite interest, but consumers are generally also greatly interested in ensuring the car is reliable, has good fuel economy, and maintains its value. Those same individual consumers probably apply entirely different values to the criteria for selecting a lawn care company.

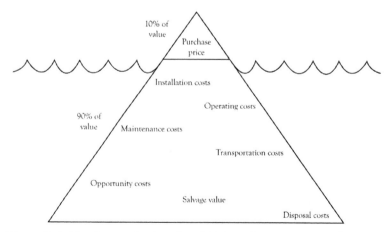

Figure 7.1. Total cost of ownership (TCO) value pyramid iceberg.

TCO models are utilized in a variety of settings to derive value. Example 7.2 is based on one of the author's experiences and introduces how TCO models were utilized by one company to assist in the decision-making process.

Example 7.2. Lighting TCO Analysis

The director of strategic procurement for a high-end specialty retailer, KT Apparel, has determined that one of the key areas of focus for the coming years should be on energy management for the company's 2,200 stores. With energy prices at near all-time highs and continued emphasis on being "green," he began to look at options that might be available to curb energy use without sacrificing the look in stores. He knows that there are two major items driving store energy costs: lighting and heating and cooling. He decides to focus his attention initially on lighting costs.

The director schedules a meeting with the preferred supplier recently selected to provide lighting solutions for their stores to discuss options for reducing energy consumption. In the meeting he shares that due to the recent downturn in the economy, his company has a limited capital budget and that he is interested in innovative solutions that might reduce operating expenditures with limited use of capital and without negatively altering the lighting in stores. Options that would enhance light levels without significant cost increases would be preferable, if available, as many store light levels are suboptimum. The supplier has come prepared to discuss a potentially attractive option KT Apparel may want to consider. They suggest replacing the existing halogen lamps with a newer, more energy-efficient model of halogen that provides greater lighting levels than the existing lamps.

The director asks for the product specification sheets for his existing halogen lamp and the alternative option for consideration. Additionally, he asks that the preferred supplier provide him a quote for the alternative lamp based on KT Apparel's historical volumes and samples of each to provide to the store design department for evaluation. The lamp specifications for each follow:

	Current halogen	Alternate halogen
Watts	60	50
Lumens	800	920
Half-life (hours)	3,000	5,000
Price	$3.15	$5.67

Over the past 3 years, the average annual expenditure for halogen lamps across all the stores is $1.2 million. The annual energy cost for all the stores combined is approximately $36 million, and a large percentage of that is believed to be consumed by inefficient lighting. Additionally, there have been a large number of insurance claims from store associates who have fallen off ladders while replacing burned-out lamps, so increasing lamp life would be doubly desirable. The director decides that a TCO model focusing on the annual cost per socket for each lamp will illustrate the best recommendation for his company to pursue going forward.

From the information presented in Example 7.2, there is considerable information the director of strategic procurement already has at his disposal to assist him in formulating a cost model. Were the director not a proactive supply chain professional, he could have easily been dissuaded from continuing to analyze this alternative based on the stark price differences between the current lamp and the alternative. However, he will use a TCO model and let the facts dictate which lamp is best for his company to adopt. In order to accurately analyze those facts, we will look at each major TCO component and then discuss its applicability for the director and KT Apparel.

Acquisition Costs

Purchase price is often what most think of when acquisition costs are discussed; however, there are a number of other components worthy of analysis as accurate TCO models are being constructed. Purchase price itself can consist of a number of elements that can differentiate options, such as negotiated price, payment terms, electronic document exchange, or warranty differences. One proposed purchase price rarely aligns exactly with another, so these items need to be entered into the TCO modeling process. Often extended warranties and early pay discount terms may be negotiated to make the acquisition cost even more attractive.

In the example we are reviewing, the option the director of strategic procurement is evaluating is from a current preferred supplier. The only price he knows is competitive is his current lamp, which was sourced within the past year. If the alternative option was proving more beneficial, he may want to take additional steps to ensure the pricing is competitive, since the halogen bulb drives a significant portion of the lighting expenditures. Example 7.3 shows how the director handles the information he has already obtained on pricing.

Example 7.3. Normalizing Lamp Life

One of the first items that caught the director's eye as he was reviewing each of the lamp specification sheets was the difference in the length of life. He knows that a half-life of 3,000 hours for the current lamp means that roughly half of those lamps produced will die before 3,000 hours and half will die after 3,000 hours. Because the half-life of the alternative lamp is significantly longer, he recognizes this as an opportunity to reduce the number of lamps purchased over a period of time and should be factored into the analysis. He decides to normalize the price of the lamps to an annualized price. To do this he first develops a multiplier to determine the number of bulbs needed per light socket if the half-life were to be assumed for all bulbs.

	Annual store hours	÷	Half life	=	Lamps consumed annually/socket
Current	4,200	÷	3,000	=	1.4
Alternate	4,200	÷	5,000	=	0.84

Then the director takes the lamps consumed multiplier and applies that to the price to develop the normalized price annually for each bulb.

	Price	×	Lamps consumed annually/socket	=	Annual normalized price/socket
Current	$3.15	×	1.4	=	$4.41
Alternate	$5.67	×	0.84	=	$4.76

With a $0.35 difference identified between the two lamp prices, he now begins to focus his attention on other components.

Installation/Implementation Costs

Installation/implementation costs are those that will be incurred for the product, service, or project to start providing the intended benefit. For products, the costs could include such things as packing materials, transportation, customs clearance, tooling, disposal costs of the product being replaced, training, and setup labor. Service and project implementation costs may include travel expenses, training, and switching costs from another provider. Example 7.4 shows how the director of strategic procurement and KT Apparel classified these costs.

Example 7.4. Installation Costs

For KT Apparel, the director and his management team decide to analyze an installation/implementation strategy for the new lamp that would be rolled out as existing lamps fail. This in effect negates any differences in large ramp-up costs between the two lamps for installation purposes. Installation procedures for the two lamps under consideration are identical and performed by the same store associates. Additionally, the packing materials, weight, and mode of shipment are comparable, so those costs are collected for inclusion in the TCO model. However, because the alternate lamp has a longer life than the current lamp, he needs to calculate the normalized annual cost for shipping per light socket.

First the director calculates the delivery price per lamp for each delivery made.

	Average case delivery price	÷	Quantity/Case	=	Average lamp delivery price
Current	$5.00	÷	12	=	$0.42
Alternate	$5.00	÷	12	=	$0.42

Then he needs to calculate what each lamp would cost annually based on the half-life calculation performed to normalize price in Example 7.3 ("Lamps Consumed Annually/Socket") to plug in to his TCO model.

	Average lamp delivery price	×	Lamps consumed annually/socket	=	Annual delivery cost/socket
Current	$0.42	×	1.4	=	$0.58
Alternate	$0.42	×	0.84	=	$0.35

The application of the multiplier illustrates a net advantage of $.23/socket annually by utilizing the alternative lamp.

Operating Costs

The impact of operating costs on the value proposition for a TCO model is often one of the larger components of cost. This is especially true with a product that consumes energy and with projects and services that consume resources during and after the life of the implementation.

For TCO analyses performed on products being sourced, such as capital equipment, ongoing operating costs can sway decision making dramatically. For example, if an energy company was looking to source a gas turbine/generator package to produce needed energy for oil field operations, the size of the unit is a huge consideration. If a package sourced produces more megawatts than is needed, the turbine/generator package also will consume more natural gas than necessary for the operation. This additional consumption of natural gas would increase operating costs dramatically and provide the operation no benefit. So even if the price of the larger turbine/generator package was lower, it might not be the best option due to increased operating costs. In this case the operation wants to fully understand the costs to operate each unit under consideration and make sure it is fit for the purpose it is intended.

In the services and projects realm, operating costs may be based on the effectiveness of the team selected to do the work. For instance, if a consulting company was being sourced to implement a new enterprise resource planning (ERP) system for the company, the sourcing team would want to ensure that the successful party had knowledge of the ERP software being implemented, knowledge of their industry, and references from previous companies on the specific individuals proposed for the implementation. If those factors are not strongly considered, and a selection is based almost exclusively on rate, the business may jeopardize implementation timelines, or worse, have to implement a number of costly workarounds to compensate for a poorly configured and tested system.

Example 7.5 follows how the director of strategic procurement and KT Apparel continue their TCO analysis by now focusing on operating costs.

Example 7.5. Operating Costs

The director's focus has been on reducing energy costs while maintaining lighting levels in stores and not dramatically increasing supply costs. The alternate bulb under consideration uses 10 watts/hour fewer than the current bulb. He knows he needs to calculate the cost per socket for each lamp to plug into his TCO model. To do that he first runs a report from his energy management system to collect the current dollar per kilowatt hour (KWh) KT Apparel's stores are being charged by location. The average cost that the stores are paying across the country is $0.10224/KWh. Though information in the marketplace shows this cost is likely to increase in the near future, the director uses this figure to conservatively model operating cost impact.

In order to calculate the KWh consumed annually by socket for each lamp, the wattage of each needs to be converted to KWs. One kilowatt is equal to a thousand watts, so the following calculation must be done for each:

	Watts per hour	÷	Watts per kilowatt	=	Kilowatts per hour
Current	60	÷	1,000	=	0.06
Alternate	50	÷	1,000	=	0.05

With the KWh calculated, the next piece to calculate is the total KWhs annually.

	Kilowatts per hour	×	Annual store hours	=	KWh's annually
Current	0.06	×	4,200	=	252
Alternate	0.05	×	4,200	=	210

To calculate the total cost per socket annually, the director must now multiply the KWhs consumed annually for each lamp times the average $/KWh the stores are charged.

	KWh's annually	×	Average $ per KWh	=	Energy cost per socket
Current	252	×	$0.10	=	$25.76
Alternate	210	×	$0.10	=	$21.47

Annually the alternate lamp being considered would provide $4.29 per socket per year in savings versus the current lamp.

Maintenance Costs

The cost to maintain the final delivered product or service is an important piece of the TCO equation. Maintenance costs for product or equipment may be based on the cost for replacement parts and the labor price and hours needed to complete the work. When we as educated consumers evaluate the best car to buy, we would consider that the upkeep cost for luxury vehicles is often much steeper than the maintenance cost for more standard automobiles. The parts and labor are generally more expensive with a luxury vehicle. So if a total cost equation was to be performed to compare two vehicles, those elements would need to be evaluated.

For services and projects, maintenance costs often are not evaluated and negotiated as diligently as the capital costs. It is not uncommon that those responsible for projects are measured solely based on whether they come in at or under the capital budget. This can often greatly impact the ongoing maintenance costs because the project manager may even use that as a tradable item in negotiations to gain a concession that meets his or her own targets. Examples of this are prevalent on large capital projects and in new software agreements. In software agreements, for example, the one-time licensing fees may be negotiated to meet the capital budget requirements, but the ongoing maintenance service expense percentage may be ignored altogether and cost the company millions of dollars over the use of the product.

Example 7.6 continues the analysis by the director of strategic procurement and KT Apparel with the focus on maintenance.

Example 7.6. Maintenance Costs

Lamp replacement is not a maintenance-intensive activity, and the time expended to replace each lamp is the same; however, the director learned early in this process that there were a number of injuries to store associates and claims associated with falls from ladders. In order to understand the potential value of fewer trips up the ladder, he requests a listing of all recordable incidents involving the use of ladders with their corresponding insurance costs while replacing lamps from human resources. From the information he receives, he can see that over the last 3 years the average value of all insurance claims pertaining to ladders and changing lamps is $250,000. Because the alternate lamp being considered has a longer life, an analysis is conducted to see how fewer trips may lead to fewer insurance claims and a safer store associate environment.

The first step to calculate this value is to determine the value across all the stores for making the switch to the alternate lamp. A calculation does not need to be done for the current lamp as the value for those annually is the $250,000 in insurance claims. The following calculations provide the multiplier to calculate the alternate lamp insurance cost:

$$\frac{\text{Alternate half-life}}{\text{Current half-life}} - 1 = \text{Percentage alternate life greater than current}$$

$$\frac{5,000}{3,000} - 1 = 0.667$$

The alternate lamp lasts two-thirds longer than the current lamp, so insurance claims should be one-third of their current costs because of the less frequent ladder use to change lamps. The following is the calculation:

$$(1 - \text{Percentage alternate life greater than current}) \times \text{Insurance claims} = \text{Alternate lamp insurance cost}$$

$$(1 - 0.667) \times \$250,000 = \$83,333.33$$

Understanding the cost per socket is the next task, and because the exact number of sockets is unknown, the director uses the purchase history he has with the current lamps consumed annually.

	Annual lamp purchase quantity	×	Lamps consumed annually per socket	=	Total sockets in stores
Current	380,892	×	1.4	=	272,066

With the number of sockets now known, the following formula can be utilized to calculate the cost per socket for each lamp:

	Annual insurance claims	÷	Total sockets in stores	=	Insurance cost per socket
Current	$250,000	÷	272,066	=	$0.92
Alternate	$83,333	÷	272,066	=	$0.31

The director will utilize the insurance cost per socket in the TCO model for each evaluated option to represent maintenance cost.

Opportunity Costs

The value to not having to perform an activity as frequently or perhaps not at all is a hidden gem when determining whether a project, service, or product is viable. In one of the examples for the operations cost portion of this chapter, we discussed how ensuring the right-sized gas turbine was placed into service could have a dramatic impact on operating costs. Utilizing that same example, the opportunity costs for making a poor decision on that type of equipment can be even more catastrophic when figuring opportunity costs. If the oil field operations generate $10 million of revenue daily and are either shut down or forced to operate at lower efficiency because of an unplanned outage in the gas turbine and generator, the lost revenue can dwarf any other cost elements considered. So for the instances of equipment critical to the business, the quality and reliability statistics of that equipment should be among the largest components of a TCO model.

In the projects and services realm earlier in this chapter, we discussed an example of selecting the right consulting firm to assist with an ERP implementation. Failure to select correctly here may impact the design of the system, impact the efficiency of the hardware, and impair users from completing business-critical tasks in a timely manner, if at all. For example, if customer lists for marketing distribution are tied to the ERP system, and those systems are not working properly, lost sales may result from the systemic problems. All those items have value that should be taken into consideration when constructing a TCO model.

For the in-depth example we are exploring in this chapter, there is a strongly identified opportunity cost that is identified to enhance the TCO model. See Example 7.7.

Example 7.7. Opportunity Costs

When looking at what the true opportunity costs are for KT Apparel to benefit from a change in lamp, the director of strategic procurement focuses on lost sales. The opportunity cost associated with store associates focusing on maintenance activities instead of selling activities is the biggest component analyzed. With the downturn in the economy, store personnel have really been cut back, so he engages store operations to understand the value that time may be worth if rededicated to selling activities.

Store operations reports back to the director: Based on a store survey, they find that associates spend approximately one hour per week changing lamps during nonpeak periods. To be conservative, they estimate that were the associates engaged in selling activities during that time frame, one additional item may be sold, based on past history. The average item selling price is $20, so a total revenue increase of $20 per store per week may be gained if that entire hour was recouped. The director knows the entire hour cannot be eliminated, but two-thirds of it can be based on his earlier work in Example 7.6. He calculates the value of that for the alternate lamp.

First, he must calculate the time per store recouped by moving to the alternative lamp by utilizing the "percentage half-life greater than current" calculation in Example 7.6 and by multiplying it by the lost sales dollars per store per week.

Percentage alternate life greater than current		Lost sales $ per week		Lost sales recouped
0.667	×	$20.00	=	$13.34

Next, the annual lost sales must be calculated for all the stores.

Total stores		Lost sales recouped		Annual weeks		Annual lost sales
2,200	×	$13.34	×	52	=	$1,526,096

The annual lost sales must then be calculated to get a per-socket cost.

$$\frac{\text{Annual lost sales}}{\text{Total sockets in stores}} = \text{Lost sales per socket}$$

$$\frac{\$1,526,096}{272,066} = \$5.61$$

A sales uplift (or opportunity cost) of $5.61 per socket will not be attained if the alternative lamp is not selected based on these findings.

Disposal and Salvage Costs

The cost components of disposal and salvage generally refer to products or equipment that have reached the end of their useful lives. For capital equipment utilized in a business operation, there is often salvage or resell value that may be recouped through its sale. For purposes of modeling cost through a piece of equipment's life, this component should be estimated while subtracting any costs incurred to generate the sale.

Many products may contain hazardous materials and require disposal in a special manner to be compliant with national and local laws. Fluorescent lamps, for example, contain high levels of mercury and are required to be disposed of through dealers or recycling companies.

Other nonhazardous products may be required to be recycled as well in some regions, such as plastic bags. The cost for collection bins, transportation costs, and any recycling fees would need to be included in a TCO model for full cost visibility.

Example 7.8 continues the TCO model for the lamp options and presents the final results.

Example 7.8. Total Cost Analysis Results

The last component to collect for completion of the total cost of ownership model is any applicable disposal costs. The director investigates and discovers that there are no governmental requirements to recycle halogen lamps and no recycle programs available. This means that the cost for disposal is a small percentage of the total costs incurred to dispose of general waste. In discussions with store operations, it is determined that the lamps occupy an infinitesimal amount of space, and removal of them from waste collection would not impact general waste costs. With no need to calculate this piece of information, the director begins to piece together his completed TCO model, placing the opportunity cost figure into the current lamp TCO model to indicate not pursuing the alternative lamp costs real money. He then places each lamp into waterfall charts for presentation to management.

The following chart is the consolidation of all the cost elements calculated for the TCO model and clearly shows the alternate lamp to be a superior option:

	Current lamp	Alternate lamp	Difference
Normalized Price	$4.41	$4.76	–$0.35
Delivery Cost	$0.58	$0.35	$0.23
Energy Cost	$25.76	$21.47	$4.29
Insurance Cost	$0.92	$0.31	$0.61
Opportunity Cost	$5.61	$0.00	$5.61
Total Annual Cost/Socket	**$37.28**	**$26.89**	**$10.39**

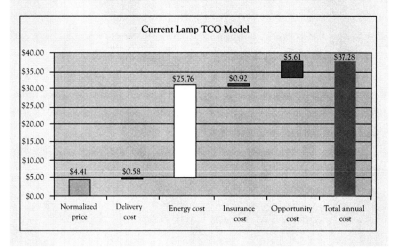

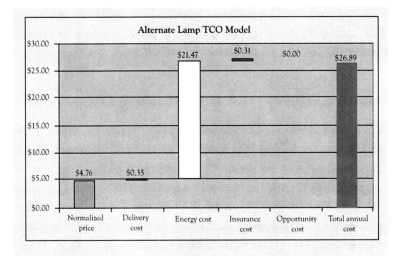

The director now has a clear picture of the total cost of ownership for staying with the current lamp or moving to the alternate lamp. When he calculates the extrapolated cost across all light sockets, he has all he needs to create a business case for change.

	Lamp TCO	×	Total sockets in stores	=	TCO cost for all stores
Current	$37.28	×	272,066	=	$10,142,610
Alternative	$26.89	×	272,066	=	$7,315,847
Annual Savings	**$10.39**	×	**272,066**	=	**$2,826,763**

Switching to the alternative lamp will save his company more than $2.8 million annually.

Conclusion

The creation of total cost of ownership models provides the most comprehensive picture as to the cost for any potential solution to the organization. The TCO model on light bulbs provides a simple insight into how TCO components can sway decision making greatly. Had the director of strategic procurement only considered energy costs and prices to construct his model, the impact of the decision would have been quite different than with the complete TCO model. It is also possible that when elements of significant cost or opportunity cost are not evaluated but the focus is on a select few elements that are easy to obtain without modeling, the decision quality will be inferior to that obtained with the TCO model. Ensuring that all elements of significance are included in the model is crucial to determining the true value of any solution.

Examining a Stream of Cash Flows: Net Present Value Analysis

When constructing a TCO model for capital equipment, which often has a lengthy useful life, it is important to evaluate the stream of cash flows associated with the ownership and operation of that equipment in current dollars. Calculating the net present value (NPV) of the stream of cash flows identified by the type of TCO analysis discussed in this chapter results in a single number that represents the value in current dollars of the entire stream of cash flows. This facilitates the comparison of alternative decisions relating to the acquisition of capital equipment.

Time

Figure 7.2. Time value of money.
The value of a dollar of cash flow decreases the farther into the future the cash flow is received.

The concept of net present value is a simple one. NPV represents today's value for a cash flow (positive or negative) that is expected to be incurred in a future period. Ask yourself, would a dollar received today be worth as much to you as the promise of a dollar to be received by you at the end of 1 year? In a period of inflation, the answer would be no because the dollar would lose purchasing power over the 1-year period. NPV answers the question of how much is the promise of a dollar to be received at the end of a year worth to an organization today. To answer this question, the analyst would calculate NPV by dividing the dollar to be received at the end of 1 year by 1 plus the inflation rate raised to the power of the number of years, n, after which the dollar will be received. Assume the current inflation rate, i, is 3% (0.03). NPV would be calculated as follows:

$$NPV = \frac{Cash\ flow}{(1+i)^n} = \frac{1}{(1+0.03)^1} = \$0.97087$$

The NPV indicates that the value of 1 dollar to be received at the end of 1 year would be $0.97087 in today's dollars.

Regardless of the inflationary climate, you could always invest today's dollar so that it would be worth more than a dollar at the end of the year. In this case, i would represent the interest rate at which the dollar could be invested rather than the inflation rate. Assuming an interest rate of 4% (0.04), the NPV would be calculated as follows:

$$NPV = \frac{Cash\ flow}{(1+i)^n} = \frac{1}{(1+0.04)^1} = \$0.96154$$

So if you had $0.96154 today and could invest it at an interest rate of 4%, the value of the investment at the end of 1 year would be 1 dollar. This calculation can easily be set up manually in a spreadsheet such as Excel. Excel will also calculate NPV by entering @NPV(rate,year1,year2, . . .) in a cell.

Consider a large gas turbine with an initial cost of $800,000 and a useful life of 5 years. It is estimated that the turbine will incur fuel, operating, and maintenance costs of approximately $75,000 per year and have a salvage value at the end of its useful life of approximately $100,000. The inflation rate is expected to be 3% during the life of the turbine. The annual cash flows would be as follows:

Year	Cash flow ($)
0	−800,000
1	−75,000
2	−75,000
3	−75,000
4	−75,000
5	−75,000 + 100,000 = 25,000

The NPV of the 5-year stream of cash flows is calculated as the following:

$$NPV = \frac{-800,000}{(1+0.03)^0} + \frac{-75,000}{(1+0.03)^1} + \frac{-75,000}{(1+0.03)^2} + \frac{-75,000}{(1+0.03)^3} + \frac{-75,000}{(1+0.03)^4} + \frac{25,000}{(1+0.03)^5}$$

$$NPV = -\$1,026,424$$

The NPV of this turbine can be compared with the NPV of alternative turbines and, assuming all other things are equal, the decision would be made to purchase the turbine with the lowest negative NPV—that is, the NPV that is closest to zero. Consider an alternative brand of turbine with a lower purchase price of $750,000, an equivalent service life, and a salvage value of $70,000, but that has annual operating costs of $100,000 per year because it is less fuel efficient and requires more frequent maintenance. The NPV of this turbine is –$1,114,163. So the lower priced turbine is not the best selection based on NPV.

Concluding Cost Modeling

Throughout this book we have discussed the construction and application of varying types of internal and external cost models. For cost modeling there is never a one-size-fits-all model for any project, operation, good, or service, but rather it is incumbent upon the cost modeler to identify those components important and applicable for evaluation within his or her own organization in order to select the appropriate type of cost model. As stated throughout the chapters, the intention of cost models is to aid in quality decision making through the utilization of facts and to provide for scenario testing. The methodology for creating and utilizing these fact-based tools in various applications should assist the reader with applying these to his or her own organization.

APPENDIX

Data Sources for Cost Modeling

Almanac of Business & Industrial Financial Ratios. http://www.cchgroup.com/webapp/wcs/stores/servlet/product_Almanac-of-Industrial-and-Financial-Ratios_10151_-1_10053_04657400

Consumer Price Index. http://www.bls.gov/cpi

Dun & Bradstreet's Industry Norms & Key Business Ratios. http://www.dnb.com/industry-norms-business-ratios-reports/14909181-1.html

IRS Publication 542 Corporations. http://www.irs.gov/pub/irs-pdf/p542.pdf

IRS Tax Statistics. http://www.irs.gov/taxstats

NAICS Association. http://www.naics.com/search.htm

North America Industry Classification System (NAICS). http://www.census.gov/eos/www/naics

Producer Price Index. http://www.bls.gov/ppi

RMA Annual Statement Studies. http://www.rmahq.org/RMA/CreditRisk/DataDecisionSupportCenter/StatementStudies

U.S. Census Bureau Annual Survey of Manufacturers. http://www.census.gov/manufacturing/asm/index.html

U.S. Economic Census. http://www.census.gov/econ

Notes

Chapter 1

1. Maloni and Benton (2000); Cox (2001); Zelbst et al. (2009).
2. Ask and Laseter (1998).

Chapter 2

1. Cokins (1996), p. 40.

Chapter 3

1. Sower (2011).
2. Cokins (1996), p. vii.

Chapter 4

1. Harrington (2004), p. 18; Arcplan (2010), p. 2.
2. Evans and Lindsay (2008), pp. 530–532; IMPO (2010), http://www
.impomag.com/scripts/ShowPR-RID-9739.asp
3. Arcplan (2010), p. 3.
4. Carr (1995), pp. 26–32.
5. Dow Chemical (1999).
6. Donovan (2006).
7. Sower et al. (2007), p. 128.
8. Campanella (1990), pp. 5–23.
9. Sower (2011), p. 314.

Chapter 5

1. U.S. Economic Census (2002).

Chapter 6

1. Freedom of Information Act (FOIA) requests may be made to any U.S. governmental agency. Though not all requests are granted, this is another excellent manner to obtain more detailed information for cost modeling. Check the agency website first to ensure the information needed is not already published, and if not, to get detailed instructions on how and where to send the FOIA request.

References

Anklesaria, J. (2008). *Supply chain cost management*. New York, NY: AMACOM.

Arcplan. (2010). *Making the business case for better supply chain quality management*. Berwyn, PA: Arcplan.

Ask, J., & Laseter, T. (1998). *Cost modeling: A foundation purchasing skill*. Retrieved June 19, 2011, from http://www.strategy-business.com/article/9625?gko=ba075

Burt, D., Norquist, W., & Anklesaria, J. (1990). *Zero base pricing*. Del Mar, CA: Byline.

Campanella, J. (Ed.). (1990). *Principles of quality costs* (2nd ed.). Milwaukee, WI: ASQ Quality Press.

Campanella, J., & Corcoran, F. (1983). Principles of quality costing. *Quality Progress 16*(4), 17–22.

Carr, L. (1995). How Xerox sustains the cost of quality. *Managerial Accounting 76*(2), 26–32.

Cokins, G. (1996). *Activity-based cost management*. Boston, MA: McGraw-Hill.

Cox, A. (2001). Understanding buyer and supplier power: A framework for procurement and supply competence. *The Journal of Supply Chain Management 37*(2), 8–15.

Dobler, D., & Burt, D. (1996). *Purchasing and supply management*. New York, NY: McGraw-Hill.

Donovan, S. (2006). *Using cost of quality to improve business results*. Retrieved from http://www.asq.org

Dow Chemical. (1999). *Annual report to shareholders*. Midland, MI: The Dow Chemical Co.

Evans, J., & Lindsay, W. (2008). *Managing for quality and performance excellence*. Mason, OH: Thompson Higher Education.

Handfield, R., & Nichols, N. (2002). *Supply chain redesign*. Upper Saddle River, NJ: Prentice Hall.

Harrington, H. (2004). Measuring money and quality. *Quality Digest 24*(2), 18.

IMPO. (2010). *Q & A with Gary Reiner of GE, and Liam Durbin of GE Fanuc*. Retrieved June 19, 2011, from http://www.impomag.com/scripts/ShowPR-RID-9739.asp

Maloni, M., & Benton, W. (2000). Power influences in the supply chain. *Journal of Business Logistics 21*(1), 49–73.

Malstrom, E. (1981). *What every engineer should know about manufacturing cost estimating.* New York, NY: Marcel Dekker.

MTM Systems. http://www.mtm.org/systems.htm

Sower, C., & Sower, V. (2009). *Getting industry-specific cost models to work for you.* Institute for Supply Management 2009 Conference Proceedings, Charlotte, NC.

Sower, V. (2011). *Essentials of quality with cases and experiential exercises.* Hoboken, NJ: Wiley.

Sower, V., Quarles, R., & Broussard, E. (2007). Cost of quality usage and its relationship to quality system maturity. *International Journal of Quality & Reliability Management 24*(2), 121–140.

U.S. Economic Census. (2002). *Industry series reports manufacturing.*

Zelbst, P., Green, K., Sower, V., & Reyes, P. (2009). The impact of supply chain linkages on supply chain performance. *Industrial Management & Data Systems 109*(5), 665–682.

Index

The letters *f* and *t* following a page number denote a figure or table respectively.

Announcing the Business Expert Press Digital Library

Concise E-books Business Students
Need for Classroom and Research

This book can also be purchased in an e-book collection by your library as

- a one-time purchase,
- that is owned forever,
- allows for simultaneous readers,
- has no restrictions on printing,
- can be downloaded as PDFs from within the library community.

Our digital library collections are a great solution to beat the rising cost of textbooks. E-books can be loaded into their course management systems or onto students' e-book readers.

The **Business Expert Press** digital libraries are very affordable, with no obligation to buy in future years.

For more information, please visit **www.businessexpertpress.com/librarians**. To set up a trial in the United States, please contact **Sheri Allen** at *sheri.allen@globalepress.com*; for all other regions, contact **Nicole Lee** at *nicole.lee@igroupnet.com*.

OTHER TITLES IN OUR SUPPLY AND
OPERATIONS MANAGEMENT COLLECTION
Series Editor: **Steven Nahmias**

A Primer on Negotiating Corporate Purchase Contracts by Patrick Penfield

Production Line Efficiency: A Comprehensive Guide for Managers by Sabry Shaaban and Sarah Hudson

Supply Chain Management and the Impact of Globalization by James A. Pope

Orchestrating Supply Chain Opportunities: Achieving Stretch Goals Efficiently by Ananth Iyer and Alex Zelikovsky

Transforming US Army Supply Chains: Strategies for Management Innovation by Greg H. Parlier

Challenges in Supply Chain Planning: The Right Product in the Right Place at the Right Time by Gerald Feigin

Design, Analysis and Optimization of Supply Chains: A System Dynamics Approach by William R. Killingsworth